Christians and Nonviolence
in the Nuclear Age

Scripture, the Arms Race, and You

PREFACE TO

CHRISTIANS AND NONVIOLENCE
IN THE NUCLEAR AGE

The American Catholic bishops' pastoral letter on war and peace, issued in May 1983, aroused a storm of controversy in both religious and political circles. It brands as immoral the central feature of American defense policy: the willingness to use nuclear weapons on population centers of enemy countries. Even the possession of these weapons as a deterrence, the bishops said, is morally acceptable only if it is used as a step toward progressive disarmament, which it certainly has not been in any presidential administration since such weapons became part of the American arsenal in 1945.

When the contents of the pastoral letter became public, people who had long taken American defense policy for granted were suddenly faced with the assertion that this policy is largely wrong. It is wrong in the sight of God, it is wrong according to the teachings of scripture, it is wrong by the measurements of moral principles.

Critics accused the bishops of incompetence, of being out of their element, of venturing into areas too complex for any but the experts. The bishops were advised to stick to religious matters and stay away from politics.

XXIII

TWENTY-THIRD PUBLICATIONS
P.O. Box 180   Mystic, CT 06355

The bishops pointed out, however, that they had extensively consulted a host of experts in drawing up their position. They said it was their duty to identify the real-life implications of moral guidelines, even when these involved the political and military.

The opening chapter of *Christians and Nonviolence in the Nuclear Age* presents the factual basis for the assessment of nuclear weapons given in the bishops' pastoral. When one understands what is meant by "mutual assured destruction," the bishops' evaluation makes sense.

The second chapter offers a theological assessment of nuclear weapons drawn from the prophetic tradition of scripture. It calls them idols.

But then we have the life and teachings of Jesus as a positive guide. Vatican Council II, as the bishops recall, urged us to evaluate war with an entirely new attitude. That new attitude helps us discover the direction Jesus would have us take, which is outlined in the book's third chapter.

The bishops' pastoral letter points out that there have been "two legitimate modes of Christian witness on issues of war and peace." One is the "just war" tradition, prominent in Catholic moral teaching for centuries. The other is Christian pacifism, or nonviolence. The pastoral observes: "Today in the Catholic community, when any issue of peace or war is addressed, the nonviolent tradition must be part of the discussion." Chapter 4 of this book presents the dynamics of nonviolence, how it works, and its potential for meeting the challenge of the Nuclear Age.

"But what about the Russians?" people ask. Chapter 5 deals with the whole idea of the Enemy, and suggests a realistic approach that should help in understanding the sober assessment of Soviet policy given by the bishops.

The challenge of the Nuclear Age, which the bishops have highlighted, is a personal one. All of us are affected, and all of us can respond creatively. The final chapter of this book outlines ways we can begin immediately to incorporate nonviolence into our daily lives as the first step in working for a more peaceful world. Along these lines we can move forward in our response to, in the bishops' words, "the gift of peace, made available to us in the Spirit of God."

—Gerard A. Vanderhaar

CHRISTIANS
AND
NONVIOLENCE
IN THE
NUCLEAR AGE

Scripture, the Arms Race, and You

Gerard A. Vanderhaar
Foreword by Bishop Carroll T. Dozier

TWENTY-THIRD PUBLICATIONS
P.O. Box 180   Mystic CT 06355

DEDICATION

In memory of all those people of peace whose inspiration and support are responsible for this book.

Edited by Amy Burman
Designed by John G. van Bemmel
Cover by William Baker

Library of Congress Catalog Card Number: 82-82388

FOREWORD

There is an adversary that entwines itself with the very concept of patriotism and smothers it. There are so many times when we cannot distinguish the real vine from the parasite.

This adversary is strong and evil. But its actions are performed with such righteousness that minds and hearts are blinded to the questions of right and wrong. These decisions are made upon a presumed position, which position is never criticized.

This adversary pretends to know and to judge right from wrong. It stands before the Decalogue of Moses and refutes the meaning of each one. This adversary reaches its height of arrogance when confronted by that commandment which says so clearly, "Thou shall not kill." This adversary calls for a reversal of that commandment, "Yes, you may kill."

When this reversal is given, the words are made more polite. In fact, they are expressed in Latin for they sound so noble. "Pro Deo et Patria" is the slogan. Or as we hear at this moment, "the Union Jack is raised again," referring to those far-off islands.

Is there any wonder that Samuel Johnson's quotation

5

is always remembered and is usually applicable: "Patriotism is the last refuge of a scoundrel"? If we care to tarry a moment over our latest international war, we would raise the question of how a nation's interest can be so far removed — 10,000 miles; and the further question of the cost of sailing so far for a place not worth the cost of sailing.

Our modern age has been asked to develop a new attitude, a new conscience toward war and its violence. When the Second Vatican Council asked this of the members of the Catholic Church, we had no idea that it would be a task of so many years and one of such depths.

Our past formation had been along the lines of a just war theory. We applied it easily, seeking always to prove the other as the aggressor and that our side had been injured. When the flag waved, off we marched. It was as American as apple pie.

Now the monstrous succession of one weapon system after another has brought us and the world, which does not belong to us but over which we do have stewardship, to the point where we can destroy it and all its people.

Do we heedlessly run along the path singing "Pro Deo et Patria" into nuclear destruction?

Or, do we turn away from the entwining of God and country? Do we see in this turning a vast difference between the things of God and the things of country?

Doctor Vanderhaar has brought us a timely book through the pages of which we can grasp the task which is ours. This task is no less than forming an entirely new conscience and developing a right attitude towards war.

The peace movement catches its meaning from the Prince of Peace who brought us peace and reconciliation and gave it to us as a gift.

+ Carroll T. Dozier, D.D.
Bishop of Memphis
June 1, 1982

CONTENTS

INTRODUCTION

My country is prepared to destroy the world. It will do this in my name, with my money, under the pretext of saving me from the Russians.

I don't want this to happen. It is not inevitable. I would like to do something to prevent it.

This means I have to examine various alternatives and decide on a course of action different from the present one. This book explores new ways of thinking, about war, about ourselves, about what we believe most deeply. It suggests that active nonviolence is an appropriate personal response to the challenges of the Nuclear Age.

Nonviolence takes two forms: a firm no to the forces that propel us on the road to nuclear destruction, and a strong yes to ways of affirming human life and dignity. It involves seeking constructive means to resolve conflicts on the personal, social, and international levels. Above all, it involves a rethinking of old patterns of reacting.

Like most Americans, I was an enthusiastic supporter of the United States actions in World War II. As a high school student I was envious of my older cousins and family friends who were in the service, proud to see them in uniform, and shocked when one was killed and another physically wrecked in a prisoner of war camp.

I was convinced then, and am still convinced today, that most of the military people who fought in World War II were motivated by patriotism and duty.

I remember being excited and thrilled when the atomic bombs were dropped on Hiroshima and Nagasaki and the Japanese surrendered a week later. They were the enemy, I felt. They had started it at Pearl Harbor, and they deserved what they got from American bombers and flame throwers.

The war had begun for us on December 7, 1941, "a date," President Roosevelt said, "which will live in infamy." It gained momentum inexorably. Winning it became an all-consuming goal for millions of Americans. When President Roosevelt and Prime Minister Churchill at Casablanca in 1943 defined winning as the unconditional surrender of the Axis powers, they in effect declared total war.

Few Americans at that time imagined that the righteous indignation against Japan for Pearl Harbor would escalate into the fury of Dresden and Hiroshima two and a half years later.

Fifty-five million people died in World War II, according to the painstaking calculations of Gil Elliot in his *Twentieth Century Book of the Dead.* Twenty million of those were Russians, victims of the Nazi invasion. Five million Germans were killed, 3 million Poles, 2.5 million Japanese, and 1.7 million Yugoslavs. Six million Jews from all over Europe perished in the death camps. Great Britain lost 460,000 people.[1] The United States death toll was 407,000.

Most of those who died were killed by people acting out of patriotism and duty. The underlying rationale was that if it is permissible to kill a single person for the sake of one's nation, then it is permissible to kill many more in order to accomplish the nation's purpose. Technological developments in weaponry and social organization of resources made mass killing possible during World War II. Fifty-five million deaths were the result.

Shortly after the war ended, doubts about the wisdom and

morality of using the atomic bombs on Japan began to surface in public. Robert Oppenheimer, the father of the atomic bomb, told President Truman, "There's blood on my hands." (The President's reaction was to instruct Secretary of State Dean Acheson, "Don't ever bring that man in here again.")[2]

The nuclear build-up in the 1950's, with the policy of massive retaliation in the event the U.S. was attacked, kept open the possibility of widespread killing.

A turning point of sorts came for me one day in August of 1963 when I visited the concentration camp at Dachau, near Munich. The barracks were still standing, some of them serving as dwellings for Hungarian refugees. I was horrified when I opened one of the oven doors in the crematorium and realized that human bodies, tens of thousands of them, had been burned here after tortuous deaths. My revulsion increased as I inspected the gas chamber and the photographs of the atrocities on display in the museum.

As I left the gates and walked to the parking lot, I thought this must never be allowed to happen again. Immediately the idea of massive retaliation flashed into my mind. What's to prevent wholesale killing again, this time with nuclear weapons?

Trying to find an answer to that question has preoccupied me since that bright August afternoon in 1963. It led me into the peace movement two years later.

I was challenged when the Second Vatican Council of the Roman Catholic Church in 1965 urged that war be evaluated "with an entirely new attitude." Since that challenge was issued, dozens of wars have involved countries of every continent and weapons of ever more refined cruelty. The nations of the world continue to spend astronomical sums, over $500 billion a year in the 1980's, on an arms race that, as we become more aware of the desperate poverty destroying many millions of lives, becomes an intolerable scandal.

It is clear that leaders of nations are not approaching war with an entirely new attitude. It is equally clear, then, that the new attitude must originate in and flow out from concerned people everywhere.

It is difficult for anyone to admit a positive liking for the death, destruction, fire, pain, suffering, mutilation, and anguish of war. Most military professionals and government leaders would identify with General Douglas MacArthur's words at the end of his career, "I am a 100 percent disbeliever in war."[3]

But social and cultural pressures in support of the war system are great. Most people cannot say no to war until they see an alternative that defends important values without mass killing.

That alternative has become more widely known and available in the second half of the 20th century: positive, nonviolent action for peace and human dignity.

Through the inspirational actions especially of Mohandas Gandhi in the liberation of India and of Martin Luther King in the struggle for the civil rights of black Americans, it is now possible to see a way of protecting what should be protected in a threatened society while at the same time respecting the humanity of the aggressors.

Now it is much clearer to me how the holocausts of the death camps and of Hiroshima can be prevented from happening again.

The point of looking back at past wars is not to denigrate the patriotic people who fought in them and who supported them at home. The point is to avoid future wars by encouraging a hard look at the phenomenon of war itself and at other, nonviolent ways of resolving international conflict. If war in the earlier part of the 20th century has been horrible, war in the last years of the century will be even worse.

Former Defense Secretary Robert McNamara once said, "Technology has now circumscribed us all with a conceivable horizon of horror that could dwarf any catastrophe that has befallen man in his more than a million years on earth."[4]

Mangled societies, brutalized warriors, broken families, poverty, and hunger are the fruits of war. The human race has eliminated cannibalism and abolished slavery, which were at times acceptable social institutions. But we have not yet done away with war.

This book grows out of the conviction that if people face the implications of nuclear weapons, and if they see an alternative that is both practical and humanitarian, they will begin to withdraw from the war system and work creatively for peace. Then the words inscribed on the memorial cenotaph at Hiroshima will be fulfilled: "Let all the souls here rest in peace. For we shall not repeat the evil."

The purpose of this book is to challenge the ways most people with a Christian background think about war, and to suggest a different, a nonviolent, approach. By outlining a positive alternative that can be practiced not only in international relations but also in one's own life, the book aims to point the way to those concrete, existential actions that can steer our world away from self-destruction toward mutual understanding and cooperation.

1 MUTUAL ASSURED DESTRUCTION

The unleashed power of the atom has changed everything except our ways of thinking.

— *Albert Einstein*

A nuclear missile can travel between the United States and the Soviet Union in less than 30 minutes. Neither side has developed an adequate defense against such missiles. In fact, the two nations formally agreed in the first Strategic Arms Limitation Treaty, in 1972, not to proceed with antimissile defense systems.

The addition of more weapons does not alter the basic equation between the two countries. They are in a state of fundamental nuclear equality, meaning that both have unrestrainable power to destroy each other. Each has, in the technical Pentagon phrase, "assured destruction capability."

The situation must be seen clearly. The ultimate defense of the two most powerful nations in the history of the world rests not on their ability to defend against each other's forces, but to put fear in each other's hearts, fear based on the promise of widespread retaliatory murder.

U.S. officials have left no doubt about the United States readiness to commit this murder. Secretary of State Alexander Haig told the Senate Foreign Relations Committee in 1981 that "if we are to deter the Soviet Union we must put at risk those things — including their military capability — which they value most."[1]

President Carter's Defense Secretary, Harold Brown, made clear what "put at risk" means: "We have — and will continue to have — survivable forces capable of massive destruction of Soviet cities and industrial potential, even after an all-out surprise attack against the United States."[2]

This policy is a direct outgrowth of the weapons and strategy developed during World War II. The weapons were atomic. The strategy was called city busting.

Ending the War

In the pre-dawn hours of Monday, August 6, 1945, three American B-29s took off from the island of Tinian in the western Pacific on a 1,500 mile flight to Japan that would begin the Nuclear Age.

Unknown to the flight crews, unknown to most Americans, officials in the Japanese government had for two months been trying to negotiate an armistice to end the war. They wanted the fighting to stop, and they also wanted to keep their emperor afterward. The Americans and the British, insisting that the surrender be unconditional, rejected the peace overtures and prepared for an invasion of Japan.[3]

It would be a costly and bloody enterprise. The Japanese

were expected to mount a fanatical defense of their homeland. Americans would suffer casualities of 30,000 dead and wounded in the first month of the invasion alone. Secretary of War Henry Stimson later wrote that he understood the total dead and wounded Americans would reach more than one million before the Japanese were finally subdued.[4]

While assembling the troops and equipment for the invasion, the Allies continued the devastation of Japan from the air. On March 9, 1945, 333 B-29s had destroyed 16 square miles of Tokyo with incendiary bombs, killing 130,000 people. The next night 313 planes, using napalm, set fire to Nagoya, Japan's third largest city. On May 23 and 25, B-29s created a fire storm that ruined another 17 square miles of the capitol, including the Tokyo Army Prison where 62 captured Allied airmen died in the flames. Four days later the bombers set fire to 85 percent of Yokahama, and by the middle of June the destruction of Osaka and Kobe was so complete that both cities were taken off the target list.

Time magazine, expressing the feeling of most Americans, described the fire bombings as "a dream come true."[5]

City Busting

American attitudes toward direct attacks on civilians had undergone a complete reversal as the war progressed. In 1939 President Franklin Roosevelt, reacting to German attacks on Polish cities, had said:

> The ruthless bombing from the air of civilians in unfortified centers of population . . . has profoundly shocked the conscience of humanity. . . . I am therefore addressing this urgent appeal to every government to affirm its determination that its armed forces shall in no event and under no circumstances undertake bombardment from the air of civilian populations.[6]

Early in the war the Germans severely bombed Coventry, Rotterdam, and London.

When the Allies finally took the air offensive in 1943, they carried the same kind of warfare to German cities. At the Casablanca Conference in January, 1943, the Combined Chiefs of Staff defined the mission of strategic air power as "the progressive destruction of the German military, industrial and economic system, and the undermining of the morale of the German people to a point where their capacity for armed resistance is fatally weakened."[7]

This meant that German cities were to be targets.

Germany's war-making potential depended heavily on its industrial capacity, most of which was concentrated in its cities. Not only the factories themselves, but the people who worked in them and lived near them became targets for the bombs.

People not directly involved in industry also became targets. If many could be killed and more terrorized, the planners thought, Germany's morale would be destroyed. Not only would this help win the war, but it would also crush Germany so thoroughly that it would not want to wage war again.

The Combined Chiefs of Staff were pursuing the goal outlined by the 19th century Prussian army officer, Karl von Clausewitz, in his influential book, *On War.* Clausewitz had written that an enemy's "military power must be destroyed, the country conquered so that it cannot produce a new military power, and even the will of the enemy destroyed."[8]

The British Chief of Air Staff, Sir Arthur Harris, popularly known as "Bomber" Harris, directed that the British Bomber Command's targets were to "the built-up areas" of Germany. General Henry H. "Hap" Arnold, U.S. Army Air Force Chief of Staff, describing American participation in what had become known as city busting, said that American airmen were following the "bloody instructions" given them by the Nazis.[9]

Allied air power, using the newly developed techniques of creating fire storms, killed 50,000 in Hamburg in August, 1943, 12,000 in Darmstadt in September, 1944, 25,000 in Berlin in February, 1945. Later that month the air attacks culminated in 155,000 deaths in Dresden.[10]

The deliberate targeting of civilians came to be accepted as an integral part of the military struggle. One of the last moral restraints on the conduct of warfare was overcome in the interests of defeating the enemy. World War II became the first truly total war.

At its height a few voices were raised in protest against the policy of deliberate targeting of civilians. Some Members of Parliament criticized the British Bomber Command on moral grounds. The Secretary of State for Air's reaction was that these remarks, and similar inquiries by religious leaders, tended to "impair the morale of the bomber crews and hence their bombing efficiency."[11] His point was clear. Moral protest was not only irrelevant, it could actually hurt the war effort.

The American Jesuit theologian John Ford wrote a provocative article in 1944 on "The Morality of Obliteration Bombing." He argued, on the basis that a good end does not justify an evil means, that the direct killing of civilians through massive air attacks was an evil that could not be made right in any way, not even by the goal of victory over the Axis powers.[12] Except for a few ripples in theological circles, his article was totally ignored.

When the capture of the Pacific island of Saipan in June of 1944 gave the United States an air base close enough to launch massive bombing raids on the heart of Japan, the same tactic of obliteration bombing was directed toward the country that had attacked Pearl Harbor.

Trinity

A team of scientists and military experts in the United States had been working steadily since the spring of 1943 on the top secret Manhattan Project.

On a remote desert mesa in northern New Mexico, across the Rio Grande from the Sangre de Cristo mountains, several hundred people, living in tight security in the little town of Los Alamos, developed a new kind of weapon that would release the energy stored in the atoms of an obscure element called uranium.

The project cost $2 billion. Sixty thousand other people had cooperated, working in unknown places like Oak Ridge, Tennessee, and Hanford, Washington. The scientists at Los Alamos, under the leadership of J. Robert Oppenheimer, a former University of California physicist, built four atomic bombs.

The first, weighing four and a half tons, was enclosed in a dark green metal case 10 feet long and 28 inches in diameter. It was sent, on July 14, 1945, from Los Alamos to San Francisco, where it was loaded on the cruiser Indianapolis for a 10-day trip across the Pacific to Tinian. The scientists who fabricated the bomb nicknamed it Little Boy. It was destined for Hiroshima.

The second, using the element plutonium, was shaped like a huge, plump balloon, 5 feet in diameter, 11 feet long. It was called Fat Man, and was exploded in a test on July 16, 1945, in New Mexico.

The test site was located near Alamagordo in a part of the desert the early Spanish settlers had called Jornada del Muerte (Journey of Death), because so many wagon trains had been lost in the dry, barren wastes. Oppenheimer named the site Trinity. Few knew why he chose that name. One confidant later said it was after a sonnet by John Donne, presumably in the hopes that God would use the atomic device to free human hearts from the evil of war.

The test bomb, detonated in the pre-dawn hours of Monday, July 16, created an incredible burst of light that flooded the surrounding mountains in eerie brilliance. The flames rose to 30,000 feet. Awed by the unexpected size of the explosion, Oppenheimer recalled a line from the Hindu religious classic, the *Bhagavad-Gita:* "I am become death, the shatterer of worlds."

The flash of light was seen for hundreds of miles. A woman in Los Alamos, 200 miles away, later wrote that it was

> a blinding light like no other light one had ever seen. The trees, illuminated, leaping out. The mountains flashing into life. Later, the long, slow rumble. Something had happened, all right, for good or ill.[13]

A blind girl, riding in an automobile near Albuquerque, 150 miles from the explosion, asked, "What was that?"

The test was considered a success.

The third bomb, another Fat Man, also using plutonium, was then sent to Tinian, now that the scientists knew how it would work. Its Trinity-like explosion would destroy Nagasaki.

The fourth atomic bomb was kept in New Mexico. It would become the first member of the U.S. nuclear stockpile.

The Decision

When the Trinity test occurred, President Harry Truman was meeting with Prime Minister Churchill and Chairman Joseph Stalin at the last summit conference of the war, in the Berlin suburb of Potsdam. Truman and Churchill were "immensely pleased" when they heard the details of the test. Truman was "tremendously pepped up." Churchill said, "The atomic bomb is the Second Coming in wrath."

Some high-ranking military officials were opposed to using the bomb on Japan. Admiral William Leahy, Truman's Chief of Staff, aside from his moral reservations, suspected that the scientists and others in the Manhattan Project wanted to see the bomb dropped only "because of the vast sums that had been spent on the project." General Hap Arnold claimed the atomic bomb was unnecessary because conventional bombing alone could end the war. General Dwight Eisenhower argued that America should avoid arousing world condemnation by using a weapon that "was no longer mandatory as a measure to save American lives."[14]

Many of the scientists who developed the bomb also had reservations. Dr. Leo Szilard, involved in the project since its beginning, submitted a petition signed by 56 of his colleagues urging that before the bomb was used the Japanese be given suitable warning and the opportunity to surrender. This advice was not followed.

President Truman's decision was never really in doubt. Although he was aware that it was, as he put it, "the most terrible bomb in the history of the world," he later said that

> the atom bomb was no "great decision." . . . There were more people killed by fire bombs in Tokyo than dropping the atom bomb accounted for. It was merely another powerful weapon in the arsenal of righteousness . . . nothing else but an artillery weapon.[15]

He wanted to use this "artillery weapon" not only to end the war by forcing the Japanese into unconditional surrender, but also, as his Secretary of State James Byrnes was understood to say, "to make Russia more manageable in Europe."[16] The imminent postwar rivalry with the Soviet Union was very much on Truman's mind.

For History

The B-29 carrying Little Boy to Hiroshima that Monday, August 6, had been named the Enola Gay, after the mother of its pilot and commander of the mission, Colonel Paul W. Tibbets. It was accompanied by an instrument plane and a photography plane. The three flight crews hoped that the Chaplain's prayer before takeoff would be fulfilled: "May the men who fly this night be kept safe in thy care, and may they be returned safely to us."[17] No one on Tinian was praying for the people asleep in Hiroshima.

After seven hours of early morning flying, the Enola Gay, at 32,000 feet, was near its target. Hiroshima, Japan's seventh largest city, was the site of a substantial army base. It had not attracted any of the flood of B-29's that had been pounding other Japanese cities for months. Hiroshima had been chosen precisely because it was one of a handful of Japanese cities that had been spared severe bombing. According to Secretary Stimson, the military planners wanted to see the effects of an atomic bomb on a relatively large and untouched city.[18]

From six miles up the area of Hiroshima looked like a map, six long, slender islands lying in the delta of the Ota River, with docks jutting out into the beautiful Inland Sea. Tibbets told his crew that their conversation was being recorded. "This is for history, so watch your language. We're carrying the first atomic bomb." Most of the crew had never heard the word atomic before.[19]

At 8:15 a.m., the Enola Gay's bomb-bay doors swung open, and the 9,000-pound Little Boy began its 45-second descent. The crew put on the special dark welder's goggles they had been issued to protect their eyes from the flash. The plane banked and turned away.

The bomb exploded 2,000 feet above the city. People on the ground under it heard nothing. They saw only the brilliant flash of light, many times brighter than the sun.

Death struck instantly. Some people were vaporized by the immense heat of the explosion. More were blown to bits by the force of the blast. Bizarre deaths awaited others. Eyewitnesses reported the horror.

Many people rushed from the centre. Their bodies were burnt. Their skin was hanging down like rags. Their faces were swollen to twice normal size. They were holding their hands to their breasts. They were walking, embracing one another and crying out with pain. Someone was walking, dragging something along. To my great surprise it was his intestines. His stomach was ripped open and it came out and he was dragging it along without knowing what he was doing.

I felt something strange with my face. Then I was shocked by the feeling that the skin of my face had come off. Ah, then, the hands and arms, too. Starting from the elbow to the fingertips, all the skin of my right hand came off and hung down grotesquely. The skin of my left hand, all five fingers, also came off.

Between the Red Cross Hospital and the center of the city I saw nothing that wasn't burned to a crisp. . . . I saw fire reservoirs filled to the brim with dead people who looked as though they had been boiled alive. In one reservoir I saw a man, horribly burned, crouching beside another man who was dead. He was drinking blood-stained water out of the reservoir. Even if I had tried to stop him, it wouldn't have done any good; he was completely out of his head.[20]

A Japanese survivor told of a group of soldiers he had seen, stumbling blindly, in unspeakable agony. Manning an antiaircraft gun, they had been looking up at the single plane flying overhead at the moment of the blast. "It was the last thing they ever saw. The savage light, brighter than a thousand suns, burned every piece of flesh from their faces. Their eye sockets were hollow."[21]

No one will ever know for sure how many people died at

Hiroshima. The Japanese said more than 100,000. The American government estimated 78,000.

President Truman announced that a new kind of bomb had been used. It "added a new and revolutionary increase of destruction on the Japanese," he said. "It is an atomic bomb. It is a harnessing of the basic power of the universe. The force from which the sun draws its power has been loosed against those who brought war to the Far East."[22]

The dead in Hiroshima included 20 American airmen in a prisoner of war camp, and 6,000 Japanese children who were on their way to school when the bomb exploded.

Hearing the news, a city official in Albuquerque, New Mexico, was quoted in the local newspaper as saying, "The good thing about the atomic bomb is that it not only kills the little devils but it buries them, too."[23]

Eighty-four thousand other people were injured at Hiroshima. Many of them would die of a strange new illness unforeseen by the Los Alamos scientists: radiation sickness. One mother said that her daughter received no wounds at all in the initial explosion, but six years later began to complain of pains in her throat and shoulder. Six days later she died.

Thirty years later, between 70 and 80 people were still dying each year from leukemia and other radiation-induced diseases.

Three days after Hiroshima, on Thursday, August 9, Fat Man was dropped on Nagasaki, killing another 30,000 Japanese.

Still the B-29 raids continued: 170 planes on August 7, the day after Hiroshima; 420 on August 8; 109 on August 9, Nagasaki day, and 110 on August 10. The Air Force launched its largest attack, 1,000 aircraft, on August 14, immediately before the Japanese surrender was accepted that day. General Carl Spaatz, commander of the Strategic Air Force, had wanted "as big a finale as possible."[24]

Surrender

The Japanese surrender on August 14 was unconditional, as the Allies had insisted. But they were allowed to keep their Emperor.

If the Allies had agreed to this one condition in June of 1945, the Japanese surrender could have been accepted then. The war would have ended without the fire bombings of the summer, without an invasion that would have cost tens of thousands of American and Japanese lives, and without the atomic bombings of Hiroshima and Nagasaki.

In retrospect it is clear that war fever had infected the leaders and people of the nations involved. Most Japanese were prepared to die in a last-ditch stand to defend their homeland against an American invasion. Japanese leaders in June, 1945, were not all agreed that they should surrender, even conditionally.

The fever contaminated the Allies, too. They refused to accept anything less than the complete crushing of the German and Japanese war machines. To this end they set out to destroy as much of these countries as possible.

In the judgment of many, Hiroshima joins Auschwitz as a symbol, in the words of historian Barton Bernstein, "of the capacity of the modern state to justify mass murder, and of the inability of most citizens, especially in time of war, to affirm the humanity of the enemy or to oppose the brutal practices of their own state."[25]

The Arms Race

When Oppenheimer in October of 1945 was awarded a scroll of appreciation for his work as leader of the Manhattan Project, he responded, "If atomic bombs are to be added as new weapons to the arsenals of a warring world, or to the arsenals of nations preparing for war, then the time will come when mankind will curse the names of Los Alamos and Hiroshima."[26]

Atomic bombs were in fact quickly added to the arsenal of the United States. The Soviet Union produced its own version in 1949. In the early 1950's both countries developed the hydrogen bomb, utilizing the much more powerful fusion technique to unleash the energy of the atom.

Hydrogen bombs with a destructive force 50 or more times greater than the Hiroshima bomb were developed. Little Boy was thought to be the equivalent of 15,000 to 20,000 tons of TNT. A new term, megaton, was coined to measure the power of hydrogen bombs. It means the equivalent of one million tons of TNT. One megaton is close to the destructive power of all the bombs used in all the wars since the invention of gunpowder, in the estimation of physicist Bernard Feld.[27]

A one-megaton hydrogen bomb instantly destroys everything within a radius of a mile and a half of where it explodes. If exploded over a city, every building in that radius would disintegrate. All living creatures would die in a fraction of a second, and disappear. Within a three-mile radius, the heat would be so severe that almost anything exposed to it would burst into flames. As far as eight miles away people would suffer second degree burns from the blast. Thirteen miles away anyone looking in the direction of the flash would be blinded.[28]

As much as one-third of the population of a city of one million people would be killed or wounded by the blast and fire of a one-megaton bomb, depending on the warning time and availability of shelter.

Bits and pieces of matter, pulverized and drawn high up into the sky, would spread out in clouds, and begin a long, silent descent to earth in the form of grey ashes, sometimes mixed with black rain, as at Hiroshima. It would begin falling on the city a few hours after the blast, killing tens of thousands more by deterioration of the blood, tissue, bone marrow, and by cancer.

Survivors would have to spend up to a month in overcrowded fallout shelters, shocked and demoralized by the enormity of the disaster. Many victims of the fallout would pass on debilitating genetic mutations to future generations.

In the 1980's, the United States and the Soviet Union possess huge quantities of these weapons. The Soviets have about 20,000 atomic and hydrogen bombs of all sizes, and the United States some 30,000. About one-third of these are called strategic, because they are intended for intercontinental use on the cities and military installations in the heart of the enemy country. The other two-thirds are labeled tactical. They are designed for shorter-range use.

Full-sized replicas of atomic and hydrogen bombs are on

display in the Atomic Museum on the grounds of Kirkland Air Force Base in Albuquerque, New Mexico. The first H-bomb was huge, nearly as big as a railroad tank car, painted a dark, gloomy green. Technological advances made the bombs smaller, eventually about the size of a torpedo. Their sleek, white, streamlined casings hint at the exotic world of technological breakthroughs rather than at boiling flesh and shattered cities.

Military research and development has produced many other kinds of nuclear weapons: air-to-air missiles for nuclear dogfights, artillery shells, antitank weapons, depth charges, and land mines small enough to be carried by two men and fit in the trunk of a car. Although some of these nuclear weapons are less destructive than the bomb that obliterated Hiroshima, most are much more powerful.

Deterrence

In addition to the two nuclear superpowers, Great Britain and France each possess several hundred of these weapons. China has fewer. India has exploded one in a test. There is serious speculation that Israel and South Africa have developed a nuclear capability, although neither nation officially admits it. Possessors of these weapons rely on the threat of annihilative retaliation to deter a would-be attacker.

When he was Secretary of Defense, Robert McNamara outlined the statistics of deterrence. We must be capable "of damaging the aggressor to the point that his society would be simply no longer viable in twentieth-century terms." This kind of destruction would be inflicted on the Soviet Union, he said, by 400 hydrogen bombs dropped on Soviet cities. Over one-third of people would be killed, and one-half of Soviet industrial capacity would be destroyed.[29]

McGeorge Bundy, an assistant to President Lyndon Johnson, thought it would take a lot less than 400 to deter. "In the real world of real political leaders — whether here or in the Soviet Union — a decision that would bring even one hydrogen bomb on one city of one's own country would be recognized in advance as a catastrophic blunder; ten bombs on ten cities would be a disaster beyond history; and a hundred bombs on a hundred cities are unthinkable."[30]

Ten bombs would be a "disaster beyond history." Four hundred can kill 30 percent of the people in the Soviet Union. The United States, with its 10,000 strategic nuclear warheads, can destroy every city in the Soviet Union of 100,000 or more people 36 times. The Soviets, with 6,000, can destroy every United States city 11 times.

People can die only once, and this capacity has become known as overkill. It is far beyond the number needed to deter any conceivable enemy. Winston Churchill once described it as the ability to "make the rubble bounce."

The United States and the Soviet Union possess a triad of swift, sophisticated nuclear attack systems for their strategic hydrogen bombs: land-based missiles, submarine-launched missiles, and long-range bombers.

Many of these missiles carry several warheads, each capable of destroying a city. Some of the bombers can launch smaller, pilot-less aircraft, cruise missiles, that skim the ground at twice the speed of sound and drop a hydrogen bomb on target.

Each of these systems in the strategic triad carries a sufficient number of nuclear bombs to destroy another nation, even if most of the weapons in the other two systems were eliminated by a surprise attack.

Too Close

U.S. officials have seriously considered using nuclear weapons a number of times since the end of World War II. President Truman told a press conference on November 30, 1950, that atomic bombs might be used against the Chinese army, which had just swept into Korea across the Yalu River. Secretary of State John Foster Dulles suggested to French Foreign Minister Georges Bidault in 1954 that two nuclear weapons be used to help the French forces that were surrounded at Dien Bien Phu in Vietnam. General William Westmorland wanted to use tactical nuclear weapons in Vietnam to relieve the siege of American forces at Khe Sanh in 1968.[31]

On one occasion the United States President took his nation so close to the brink of nuclear war that the decision to prevent it had to be taken not by American officials, but by the leaders of the Soviet Union. It happened during the Cuban missile crisis in 1962. Attorney General Robert Kennedy recounted the details in his book, *Thirteen Days*.[32]

The United States had imposed a military blockade on Cuba, and had ordered the Soviet Union to withdraw its missiles from that country. On the twelfth day of the crisis two letters were received from Soviet Premier Nikita Krushchev. The first said that the Soviet Union would withdraw its missiles if the United States would stop the blockade and promise not to invade Cuba. The second letter added a third condition: the United States must dismantle and remove its own missiles from Turkey, on the Soviet border.

In fact, the missiles in Turkey were obsolete. Their targets had been taken over by submarines, and there was no more use for them. Several months earlier President John Kennedy had instructed Secretary of State Dean Rusk to tell the Turkish government these missiles were going to be removed. But the Turkish officials had resisted the removal, and Secretary Rusk had not pressed the case.

The confrontation with the Soviet Union, then, came to this: Krushchev proposed three conditions. Kennedy was willing to accede to the first two, but not the third, because, he said, he did not want to seem to be bowing to Soviet pressure.

Kennedy's reply to Krushchev agreed to the first two conditions, but it did not mention the third. He sent his brother Robert to the Soviet Ambassador in Washington to make sure the Soviets knew he did not agree to the third condition.

Feeling that Krushchev would probably not accept this solution, Kennedy then ordered preparations for an invasion of Cuba to destroy the missile bases directly. Kennedy and his advisors anticipated that 25,000 American lives would be lost in the invasion, Soviet military personnel would be killed, and the Soviet Union would retaliate by attacking Berlin or Turkey. They fully expected World War III to begin.

With the decision now in his hands, Chairman Krushchev accepted Kennedy's reply, did not press his third condition, ordered Soviet ships to turn back before they encountered the blockade, and promised to remove the missiles from Cuba.

World War III was averted in 1962 because the Soviet leaders refused to go as far as the United States leaders in precipitating it.

But in the 1980's both sides are poised for it.

The nuclear policy of the United States was outlined at the first Special Session on Disarmament of the United Nations. Walter Mondale, then Vice-President, said that his government is prepared to use these weapons in the event of an attack on "the United States, our territories, or armed forces, or . . . our allies."

The Soviet statement on the same occasion was somewhat more restrained, but the threat was equally obvious. Foreign Minister Andrei Gromyko told the U.N. that the Soviet Union could use nuclear weapons in the event of aggression against "ourselves or our allies by another nuclear power." He directed the Soviet nuclear threat only against other nuclear powers. Conventional military might, he suggested, was sufficient to deal with non-nuclear countries.

Most officials hope nuclear weapons will never have to be used. Former Secretary of State Rusk said, "They must be regarded as weapons of the last resort, on which lies a curse." The first nation to use them "will carry the mark of Cain on its brow for the rest of history."[33]

When he was President, Jimmy Carter acknowledged that shame and guilt would accrue to any nation that uses these weapons. "I think anyone recognizes that the first nation to use atomic weapons would be taking a very profound step toward self-condemnation of the whole world," he said.

Blow Up the World

In the 1970's, the United States succeeded in refining the accuracy of its nuclear arsenal so that a missile launched halfway around the world could land within a few hundred feet of its target. This gave the possibility of direct hits on Soviet missile sites, as well as a more confident pinpointing of all other targets, military and civilian.

In the event of a Soviet attack, U.S. decision makers do not have to order immediate destruction of Soviet cities. They can choose instead to "take out," say, only the enemy's missile sites or airfields. If the Soviet Union responded with a similar strike, as it most likely would, the war would quickly escalate.

A colonel at the Army War College's National Security Seminar in 1975 described the prevailing military attitude toward nuclear weapons. If war breaks out, he said, "we'll fight with conventional weapons, until we're losing. Then we'll use tactical nuclear weapons, until we're losing. Then we'll blow up the world."

An all-out nuclear exchange would involve as many as 250 million deaths, and the complete destruction of the countries involved.

The prospect of blowing up the world, regrettable as it is, is justified by some on the grounds that it would totally destroy an enemy who had totally destroyed us. "Unlimited nuclear war could be justified as the most desperate of desperate measures," acknowledged Georgetown University Government Professor William V. O'Brien. "A decision to engage in such a war would be made not so much in virtue of the military necessities of 'winning' the object of the conflict, but rather in virtue of the desire to deny the victor the fruits of his victory."[34]

There Is Hope

The extremely destructive nature of nuclear warheads, the large quantities of them in existence, and the persistent tendency to think of them as just another weapon, make the threat of destruction of civilization greater than at any time in the history of the world.[35]

Because the threat has existed for four decades, and because it is not constantly thrust into the foreground of world consciousness, most people have come to accept it like the threat of an earthquake or a volcano. If nuclear war broke out it would, to this way of thinking, be what insurance companies call an Act of God.

But the difference is considerable. Earthquakes and volcanoes are convulsions of nature totally beyond human control. Nuclear weapons, their delivery systems, and the international relations that threaten their use are totally within human control.

And herein lies hope. Those who build and those who brandish these weapons act out of particular understandings and emotional configurations. The people can change.

2   NUCLEAR IDOLATRY

The taproot of violence in our society today is our intent to use nuclear weapons. Once we have agreed to that, all other evil is minor in comparison.

—*Richard T. McSorley*

Twenty years after Hiroshima, the Second Vatican Council of the Roman Catholic Church condemned the kind of warfare made possible by nuclear weapons. In a sober assertion reflecting the convictions of almost all of the 2,500 Catholic bishops from all over the

33

world, the Council declared, "Any act of war aimed indiscriminately at the destruction of entire cities or of extensive areas along with their population is a crime against God and man himself. It merits unequivocal and unhesitating condemnation."[1]

This, the only condemnation that became part of the record of Vatican II, was motivated by the nuclear devastation of Hiroshima and Nagasaki, and the post-war targeting of many cities in other parts of the world for even worse fates. Such destruction deserves complete condemnation. No rationale can justify it, no precedent can excuse it, no results can exonerate it.

The verdict is in. The judgment is clear. The kinds of weapons the United States and some other countries have been building and deploying in the name of national security are immoral, inhumane, cruel, despicable, and frighteningly dangerous to the future of the human race.

But despite common sense, despite the pleas of Popes, poets, and pundits, despite deep human instincts toward fostering life, not destroying it, this insane "defense" program goes ahead. It is in direct contradiction to God's command to choose life, to Jesus' way of love of enemy, and to the whole humane thrust of compassion for the weak and suffering.

The biblical image that most fittingly categorizes such a deviation from God's laws and human dignity is idolatry, the worship of false gods.

Paul Tillich defined the essence of religion as "ultimate concern." His phrase helps identify what the people of a nation worship, that is, what they look to for protection, what they are willing to sacrifice other national goals for, what they turn to for their safety and security, their earthly salvation.

When a president lowers spending for social programs while increasing the money given to defense, he highlights the nation's ultimate concern. When an administration receives Congressional approval to spend a trillion and a half dollars over five years to "rearm America," which is already armed to the teeth, it reflects what in fact is the country's ultimate concern.[2]

Religiously sensitive Americans perhaps feel uncomfortable

with labeling the national attachment to missiles and warheads and nose cones and jet fighters and tanks and napalm and nerve gas as the worship of false gods. But as long as a nation relies on these instruments of death for its security, its people are committing idolatry as clearly as the Israelites of old when they turned away from the Covenant and put their trust in alien gods.

The Idols

Pentagon procurers, perhaps unwittingly, have underscored this idolatry by giving some of their weapons the names of ancient gods. America's first strategic missile, developed in the late 1950's, was called Jupiter. This Roman deity, god of light, god of the sky, was chief among all the Roman gods, protector of the Roman Empire. America's Jupiter was an intermediate-range ballistic missile, installed in the NATO countries of Greece and Turkey. It was designed to strike through the sky and explode with the light of the sun over cities in the Soviet Union.[3]

America's next high god was Thor, a missile with a 1,500-mile range, deployed in Great Britain in the early 1960's. The original Thor, after whom the fifth day of the week is named, was a German god of thunder. He was also a god of war. The ancient Germans invoked his name and chanted his praises when they marched into battle against Caesar's legions.[4]

The Air Force's first intercontinental missile was given the name Atlas. The Atlas of old was one of a race of giants called Titans, descendants of the sky god. Atlas joined with other Titans to fight against Zeus. They lost, and Atlas was condemned to carry the heavens around on his shoulders as a punishment. Fortunately, the American Atlas was retired in 1965, before it had a chance to do battle with Zeus or anyone else.

But other Titans are very much on active duty. They are the giants of the intercontinental missiles, each carrying a 10-megaton warhead, capable of obliterating a good-sized city. More than 50 Titan missiles wait in silos in Arkansas, Kansas, and Arizona. One of the silos exploded in 1980 in Arkansas, killing an American serviceman. Fifteen years earlier another Titan in Arkansas caught fire and killed 53 civilian workers. These Titans, like the giants of old, already have a substantial kill record.

In the late 1950's the Air Force had a strategic bomber, the B-70, that bore the name Valkerie. The ancient Germans knew the Valkeries as helmeted goddesses who decided which warriors would be killed in battle. Some American airmen were killed in accidents by modern Valkeries.

Another weapon-god is called Poseidon. It is a nuclear submarine. The Greek Poseidon was god of the sea and the lord of earthquakes. The Romans called him Neptune. The modern Poseidons are sophisticated undersea machines. Their 10 MIRVed missiles carry 14 warheads apiece. Any one of those warheads will cause a fair-sized earthquake around its target area.

The Navy's newest nuclear submarine is called the Trident, which the ancients knew as the three-pronged spear carried by Poseidon/Neptune, symbol of his earth-shaking power. America's Trident is a sea monster weighing 18,700 tons, able to fire 24 missiles, each carrying 17 independently targetable warheads. One such submarine, when fully armed, can destroy 408 separate cities. These Tridents can do Neptune's dirty work very nicely. The United States Navy has plans for 30 of them.

Two other famous gods of old figure prominently in these modern idols that disgrace the land, sea and air today: Uranus, after whom the key element of the nuclear age, uranium, is named, and Pluto, invoked whenever plutonium is mentioned.

Uranus was the ancient Greek sky god, the personification of the heavens, father of the Titans. Among other unsavory characteristics, Uranus hated his children. He enjoyed throwing them into Tartarus, a place lower and darker than Hades. He would have been delighted with Hiroshima, and with Mutual Assured Destruction.

Pluto was god of the underworld. His namesake today is a deadly by-product of nuclear energy and the key component in most nuclear weapons. Pluto was also the god of wealth, because gold came from his domain under the earth. He would fittingly preside over today's nuclear extravagances, which consume huge amounts of wealth.

God's Command

Over the last 35 years the United States has looked for its safety and security to Jupiter and Thor, the Valkeries and Titans, Atlas and Poseidon, Uranus and Pluto. They are leading the world to disaster.

Biblical texts dealing with idolatry prove considerably helpful in interpreting the modern variety, and in providing guidance on what to do about it. The book of Exodus contains the key passage, God's words on Mount Sinai: "I am Yahweh your God who brought you out of the land of Egypt, out of the house of slavery. You shall have no gods except me" (Ex. 20:1-3).[5] This is the fundamental Judaeo-Christian commandment. No other gods are to be worshipped.

"You shall not make yourself a carved image or any likeness of anything in heaven or on earth beneath, or in the waters under the earth; you shall not bow down to them or serve them" (Ex. 20: 4-5a). Physically bowing down is one form of worship. Serving idols by devoting time, technique, and talents to them is another.

"For I, Yahweh your God, am a jealous God, and I punish the Father's faults in the sons, the grandsons, and the great-grandsons of those who hate me" (Ex 20: 5b). Radiation poisoning and genetic mutations are passed on to subsequent generations, as though they were God's punishments for the world's contemporary nuclear idolatry.

God's words conclude with a pledge of support for those who are faithful to him. "But I show kindness to thousands of those who love me and keep my commandments" (Ex. 20:6).

According to the account in Exodus, while Moses was receiving this and the other commandments from God, his people were making an idol to worship. In their anxiety for security, they gave their gold to have an idol they could see, a god they felt would lead them and protect them:

When the people saw that Moses was a long time before coming down the mountain, they gathered round Aaron and said to him, "Come, make us a god to go at the head of us; this

Moses, the man who brought us up from Egypt, we do not know what has become of him." Aaron answered them, "Take the gold rings out of the ears of your wives and your sons and daughters, and bring them to me." So they all took the gold rings from their ears and brought them to Aaron. He took them from their hands and, in a mould, melted the metal down and cast an effigy of a calf. "Here is your God, Israel," they cried, "who brought you out of the land of Egypt" (Ex. 32:1-4).

When Moses came down from the mountain and saw the golden calf, his first reaction was anger. "He seized the calf they had made and burned it, grinding it into powder which he scattered on the water" (Ex 32:19-20).

Moses' rage is the prototype of the anger felt today by many peace activists who, frustrated by the unyielding momentum of the nuclear arms buildup, want to lash out and smash some of the weapons.

But Moses soon cooled down. Anger was followed by anxiety. He loved his people, and feared their idolatry would lead to their destruction. He went back to God to plead for them.

Moses returned to Yahweh. "I am grieved," he cried, "this people has committed a grave sin, making themselves a god of gold. And yet, if it pleased you to forgive this sin of theirs! But if not, then blot me out from the book that you have written." Yahweh answered Moses. "It is the man who has sinned against me that I shall blot out from my book. Go now, lead the people to the place of which I told you. My angel shall go before you but, on the day of my visitation, I shall punish them for their sin" (Ex. 32:31-34).

God remained firm. He would do nothing just yet, but on the day of his visitation he would mete out the appropriate punishment. Idolatry would have its unfortunate consequences.

Israel's Sin

Despite this early warning, the Israelites throughout their history were tempted to worship other gods. Sometimes they succumbed. They were seduced by Baal, the Canaanite fertility god (e.g., Hos.

2:10), Molech, god of the Ammonites, to whom children were sacrificed (Lev. 20:2-5), Chemosh, god of Moab, once worshiped by Solomon (I Kings 11:7), Amon, the high god of Egypt (Jer. 46:35), Tammuz, the Babylonian god of vegetation (Ez. 8:14), and Ishtar, mother goddess of Babylon, whom Jeremiah called the Queen of Heaven (Jer. 44:17).

The great prophets castigated the people for their idolatry. It was the most serious of sins because it took them away from the path revealed by God, the way of living according to God's laws. Always, as they spoke God's words, the prophets linked idolatry to disaster.

> Some immolate an ox, some slaughter a man, some sacrifice a lamb, some strangle a dog. Some offer oblations of pig's blood, some burn memorial incense, some consecrate idols. Since they elect to follow their own ways and their souls delight in their abominations, I in my turn will select hardships for them and bring them what they dread (Is. 66:3-4).

Isaiah's image of an insensitive people plowing ahead despite warnings applies as much to the nuclear age as it did to his. People of his day dreaded conquest by foreign enemies. People today dread a nuclear holocaust.

The idols themselves are doomed realities, according to God's words through another prophet:

> Out of their silver and gold they have made idols, which are doomed to destruction. I spurn your calf, Samaria, my anger blazes against it. How long will it be before they purge themselves of this, the sons of Israel? A workman made the thing, this cannot be God! Yes, the calf of Samaria shall go up in flames. They sow the wind, they will reap the whirlwind (Hos. 8:4-7).

Jeremiah revealed that God would turn a deaf ear to the pleas of idolaters when they begged him for help in time of trouble:

> Yahweh said to me, "Plainly there is a conspiracy among the men of Judah and the citizens of Jerusalem. They have reverted to the crimes of their ancestors who refused to listen to my

words; they too are following alien gods and serving them. The House of Israel and the House of Judah have broken my covenant which I made with their ancestors. And so—Yahweh says this—I will now bring them a disaster which they cannot escape; if they invoke me I will not listen to them. The towns of Judah and the citizens of Jerusalem can go and invoke the gods to whom they burn incense, but these will be no help at all to them in the time of their distress" (Jer. 11:9-12).

Other sacred writers of the Hebrew Scriptures were equally clear that idolatry led to destruction:

The worship of unnamed idols is the beginning, cause, and end of every evil. Either that, or they rave in ecstasy, or utter false oracles, or lead lives of great wickedness, or perjure themselves without hesitation; for since they put their trust in lifeless idols they do not reckon their false oaths can harm them. But justice will overtake them on two counts: as idolaters, for degrading the concept of God, and as frauds, for swearing in despite of truth, in defiance of all that is holy (Wis. 14:27-30).

To show the absurdity of idolatry the sacred writers sometimes mocked the lifeless images in which so much confidence had been placed:

Their wooden gods plated with gold and silver are like a scarecrow in a melon patch—protecting nothing. Again, their wooden gods plated with gold and silver are like a thornbush in a garden—any bird may perch on it (Letter of Jeremiah, Baruch 6:69-70).

Today's nuclear idols are made with titanium and platinum, much more precious than gold and silver. The aging aircraft and mute missiles, like Jeremiah's scarecrow, protect nothing. Instead, they amplify insecurity.

Idol makers exercise considerable skill for a worthless goal:

Take a woodcutter. He fells a suitable tree, neatly strips off the bark all over and then with admirable skill . . . he gives it a human shape, or perhaps he makes it into some vile animal, smears it with ochre, paints its surface red, coats over all its blemishes. He next makes a worthy home for it, lets it into the wall, fixes it with an iron clamp. Thus he makes sure that it will not fall down—he is well aware it cannot help itself, it is only an image, and it needs to be helped (Wis. 13:11, 13-16).

The Psalmist had a message for the modern military-industrial complex that produces the nuclear gods:

Pagans' idols, in silver and gold, products of human skill, have mouths, but never speak, eyes, but never see, ears, but never hear, and not a breath in their mouths. Their makers will end up like them, and so will anyone who relies on them (Ps. 135:15-18).

People today, living in the shadow of the bomb, are in the same position as the inhabitants of Jerusalem at the time of Jeremiah:

When you tell this people all these words and they ask you, "Why has Yahweh decreed this appalling disaster for us? What is our crime? What sin have we committed against Yahweh our God?" Then you are to answer, "It is because your ancestors abandoned me—it is Yahweh who speaks—and followed alien gods, and served and worshipped them. They abandoned me and did not keep my law. And you for your part have behaved even worse than your ancestors" (Jer. 16:10-11).

Minigods

Not all idols of armament in the Eighties bear the names of exalted Greek, Roman, or German gods. Some, like idols in Israel, have the likenesses of animals.

The Sidewinder, an air-to-air missile, is also the name of a desert rattlesnake. One air-to-ground missile is called a Hound Dog. The Terrier is a surface-to-air missile used at sea. The Hawk is a surface-to-air missile used on land. The Cobra is an attack helicopter. An advanced version of the F-4 Phantom jet is called the Wild Weasel.

Some war idols have personal names: the Pershing, one of the new NATO missiles; the Honest John, a battlefield nuclear strike rocket; the Huey helicopter, the SAM surface-to-air missile, the Ethan Allen, a class of submarines. The Minuteman, hero of the Revolutionary War, is now, because of its multiple warheads and pinpoint accuracy, the most fearsome intercontinental missile on earth.

Other of these mini-gods are called by impersonal letters and numbers, appropriate to an age of high technology: the B-52 strategic bomber, the M-X super-missile, the F-111 fighter-bomber, the M-16 automatic rifle, the C-5A transport, and the new main battle tank that plagues its users by its overly complicated mechanics, the M-1.

The anonymous author of the book of Wisdom wrote about other users of similar pitiful products of human hands:

Wretched are they — in dead things putting their hopes — who have given to things made by human hands the title of gods, gold and silver, finely worked, likenesses of animals, or some useless stone, carved by hand long ago (Wis. 13:10).

The Hebrew Scriptures, the Old Testament, always portrayed idolatry in Israel as the religious worship of some tangible object instead of Yahweh, God. The rational foundation and political implications of these religious acts were not spelled out.

The Hebrews were a people with a common purpose and sense of mission. They had a land to conquer, a nation to create, and a cultural heritage to pass on. Conquest of the land was hampered by compromise with the people who lived there first, the Canaanites. The most important Canaanite god was Baal, lord of the fields, often represented by the image of a calf. For an Israelite, to worship Baal was to join forces with the Canaanites, and impede the conquest of the Promised Land.

In forging the bonds of a nation, the Israelites had to resist the influences and military pressures of other nearby peoples. The Moabites, Ammonites, and Jebusites all had their gods. Worship of foreign gods was often a code word for collaboration with the enemy.

The Israelites cherished a memory of liberation from slavery, and a promise of shalom, a peace-filled, sharing, equitable society. At their best moments they knew that these were dreams in which all people would share because — and this was their big breakthrough in the history of religion — liberation and peace were gifts of the one and only God, who was both their special God and the lord of the whole world. Dalliance with other gods weakened the vision entrusted to them.

The constraints against idolatry were not the temperamental outbursts of a jealous Yahweh, but necessary safeguards to the Israelites' political, national, and cultural identity. Idolatry, in fact, was self-destructive of them as a people.

Nuclear idolatry is self-destructive today for the people who practice it. Nuclear weapons have decreased security, increased the likelihood of nuclear war, and corrupted the society that possesses them.

Progressive Insecurity

The nuclear arms race directly decreases the security of any country engaging in it. As a country acquires more nuclear weapons, its prospective enemies feel the need to increase their own stocks. The more weapons an enemy requires, the more targets can be struck in the first country. Security is lessened with every additional nuclear weapon built.

The arms race, as the Second Vatican Council noted, is "an utterly treacherous trap for humanity."[6]

Besides decreasing security by increasing the threat from a potential enemy, the proliferation of these weapons heightens the dangers of nuclear war starting from regional conflicts. Their possession by at least six and probably eight countries puts strong pressure on others to develop their own, especially in areas like the Middle East and southern Africa where some nations feel surrounded and outnumbered by hostile powers. As more nations obtain the weapons, the likelihood that they will be used in local wars increases. Big power involvement would inevitably follow, with disastrous results.

The holocaust could also start from accident, or miscalculation.

In the early 1960's, an early warning radar system in Canada picked up what looked like several hundred Russian planes heading for the United States. A red alert was declared, American bombers took off for retaliatory strikes on Moscow and other cities in the Soviet Union. Then the approaching planes disappeared from the radar screens. The Defense Department concluded that what had looked like Russian aircraft was actually a flock of geese. The U.S. bombers were called back.[7]

Another near miss occurred in November of 1979 when a wrong tape was placed into the North American Air Defense Command's computer system. The tape, from a war game, showed missiles and bombers had been launched from the Soviet Union and were on their way to U.S. targets 15 to 25 minutes away. An alert was immediately called. Ten jet fighters scrambled to intercept the bombers before officials detected the error, after 6 minutes. If the alert had lasted one minute longer, the president and top military officials would have been notified. The president then would have had to decide whether to launch U.S. missiles immediately or risk their being destroyed in their silos.

Two similar accidents in June of 1980 included submarine-launched missiles in the warning. The alerts lasted for 3 minutes before satellites verified that there was no attack, only computer error.

These near misses underline the warning given by more than 100 American religious leaders in a 1978 Call to Faithfulness: "Nuclear war is becoming an increasingly likely event."

Self-Corruption

Even before that war starts, nuclear weapons have a corrosive effect on their possessors. As Richard Barnet, Director of the Institute for Policy Studies and a former State Department arms control advisor, observed, nuclear arms imply "that we can feel secure only if we constantly dramatize the threat of genocide. . . . The hideous irony is that there are enormous spiritual and economic costs to basing security on the threat to commit mass murder."[8]

Jesuit theologian Richard McSorley has pointed out some of these costs. Living with the intention to commit mass murder is psychologically disturbing and morally corrosive. A nation with this burden on its conscience can expect a severe deterioration of its internal morality. Its citizens will much more easily rationalize lesser crimes. "Until we squarely face the question of our consent to use nuclear weapons, any hope of large scale improvement of public morality is doomed to failure." He concludes that, in traditional Catholic language, "It's a sin to build a nuclear weapon."[9]

In the terse phrasing of the 1978 Call to Faithfulness, "To build weapons of such destruction and to be ready to use them are marks of a people losing their minds and souls."

The Lesson

Despite the prophets' warnings that God was very displeased, and that they should repent and turn away from their false gods, the people of Israel persisted in their idolatry. And they were destroyed, their nation was defeated, Jerusalem fell, the Temple was burned, and a few thousand inhabitants of Judea were taken into captivity in Babylon.

And of course the modern idols, the Titans and Tridents and Minutemen are powerless to save their modern worshippers, as Baal and Molech and Amon were powerless to save the Israelites. They are false gods.

The first responsibility of a religiously and humanely sensitive person in the nuclear age, then, is to turn away from these idols back to the ways of the Lord. Stop making Sidewinders and Hawks and Wild Weasels. Stop paying for M-X's and F-111's and M-1's. Choose instead life-enhancing occupations, life-supporting economies.

Human hands have fashioned these idols: human hands can dismantle them. In threatening the destruction and contamination of the planet believed by millions to be jewel of God's creation, they are a perversion of worship.

Jesus showed his displeasure with a perversion of worship in his day when he drove the money changers out of the Temple. Immediately afterwards, Matthew tells us, "there were also blind and lame people who came to him in the Temple, and he cured them" (Matt. 21:14).

The Temple today, that area of life in which one's ultimate concern is exercised, ought to be a place of healing, not hurting, of zeal for the ways of the Lord, not the pursuit of power and pride and profit.

Paul praised those Christians in Thessalonika who "broke with idolatry when you were converted to God and became servants of the real, living God" (I Thess. 1:9-10). He considered rival spirits, whom he sometimes called the Principalities and Powers (Col. 2:15), as dangers to the primacy of Jesus Christ. "Make sure that no one traps you," he wrote to the Colossians, "and deprives you of your freedom by some secondhand, empty, rational philosophy based on the principles of this world instead of on Christ" (Col. 2:6).

Paul had firsthand experience of the defensiveness and even violence that can be roused when idols are threatened. In a scene reminiscent of the angry response to the burning of draft files during the Vietnam era, and the destruction of nose cones at the General Electric plant in Pennsylvania in 1980 (both actions of idol smashing) the Acts of the Apostles describes the reaction of some Ephesians when they felt their goddess Diana was threatened:

A silversmith called Demetrius, who employed a large number of craftsmen making silver shrines of Diana, called a general meeting of his own men with others in the same trade. "As you men know," he said, "it is on this industry that we depend for our prosperity. Now you must have seen and heard how, not just in Ephesus but nearly everywhere in Asia, this man Paul has persuaded and converted a great number of people with his argument that gods made by hand are not gods at all. This threatens not only to discredit our trade, but also to reduce the sanctuary of the great goddess Diana to unimportance. It could end up by taking away all the prestige of a goddess venerated all over Asia, yes, and everywhere in the civilized world." This speech roused them to fury, and they started to shout, "Great is Diana of the Ephesians!" The whole town was in an uproar and the mob rushed to the theatre dragging along two of Paul's Macedonian travelling companions, Gaius and Aristarchus . . . By now everybody was shouting different things (Acts 19:24-29, 32).

The story ends with the town clerk eventually calming the crowd and averting a riot by assuring them that Diana was indeed great and that their business was not under any serious threat. Paul left town quickly after the disturbance died down.

Other New Testament writers also reacted strongly in the face of idolatry. John, in the book of Revelation, identified the most dangerous adversary of the Christians as a prostitute, sitting on a scarlet beast full of blasphemous names, a woman drunk with the blood of the saints.

John's message was to stay away from her, the prostitute, the Roman Empire. Do not fool around with her. Remain faithful to the Lamb, to Christ. Those who stood firm in the face of the Empire's immoral might will enter the heavenly Jerusalem. Those who consorted with this false god, those idolaters, John lists along with other sinners who are lost:

Happy are those who will have washed their robes clean, so that they will have the right to feed on the tree of life and can come through the gates into the city. Those others must stay outside: dogs, fortune-tellers, and fornicators, and murderers, and idolaters, and everyone of false speech and false life (Rev. 22:14-15).

God's Armor

The religious believer is called to rely on the power and faithfulness of the true God instead of on the destructiveness and threats of the false nuclear gods. Paul outlined the support his readers would have during times of trouble. Their defense (God's armor, he called it) is different from the weapons engineered by the world:

Stand your ground, with truth buckled round your waist, and integrity for a breastplate, wearing for shoes on your feet the eagerness to spread the gospel of peace, and always carrying the shield of faith so that you can use it to put out the burning arrows of the evil one. And then you must accept salvation from God to be your helmet and receive the word of God from the Spirit to use as a sword (Eph. 6:10-13).

These weapons, truth, integrity, eagerness to spread the gospel of peace, salvation from God, and the word of God from the spirit, can turn a country and a world around, change it from the way of nuclear madness and death to the way of human life and hope.

When the outcome is uncertain and the road is hazardous, strength comes from basic beliefs. The first belief follows from the recognition of where today's false gods are leading. Daniel Berrigan, the Jesuit priest and peace activist, presented it clearly at his trial in 1981 for destroying nuclear nose cones.

It's terrible for me to live in a time where I have nothing to say to human beings except, "Stop killing." There are other beautiful things that I would love to be saying to people. There are other projects I could be very helpful at. And I can't do them. I can't.

Because everything is endangered. Everything is up for grabs. Ours is a kind of primitive situation, even though we would call ourselves sophisticated. Our plight is very primitive from a Christian point of view. We are back where we started. Thou shall not kill; we are not allowed to kill. Everything today comes down to that—everything.[10]

The first step is to stop traveling the present path, no matter how many others are plunging along on it. The second step is to reestablish the direction of one's life according to the true God and his word in the world.

3 SCRIPTURE THROUGH PEACE EYES

He who was seated on the throne said, "I am making every thing new!"

— *Revelation 21:5*

"In light of my faith I am prepared to live without nuclear weapons in my country." The tens of thousands of persons who signed this pledge in the early 1980's had a conviction that God's way to peace was incompatible with the nuclear arms race. All who share this conviction can find support, encouragement, and a sound foundation for it in the Christian and Hebrew Scriptures.

The person who reads the bible with what Richard McSorley calls "peace eyes" will quickly discern its message of suffering love and hunger for justice, its teaching about a nonviolent path to peace.

For a Christian, the key to understanding the bible is the spirit of Jesus. His life and teachings are decisive in interpreting everything in it.

Jesus lived at a time of violence, the oppressive violence of foreign rule, and the reactive violence of those who would overthrow that rule.[1]

The Rulers

Jesus' homeland during his lifetime was under Roman occupation. The fiercely independent spirit of his people was kept in check by the armed might of the Roman legions. Those whose ancestors had fought for their freedom against Philistines, Egyptians, Assyrians, Babylonians, and Greeks were now reluctantly living under the Roman yoke.

Jesus lived in a conquered country. Roman money was the coin of exchange. Taxes had to be paid to Caesar. Roman soldiers were garrisoned in strategic locations, ready to put down any stirrings of discontent.

These legionnaires were a special breed. A few of them were born in Italy, but most came from the conquered tribes of western Europe, Africa, or the Middle East. If they were not already Roman citizens, they were given this honor when they signed on for their near-lifetime terms of 20 years of active duty followed by 5 more in the reserves. Few could speak Aramaic, the language of Jesus' homeland.[2]

As citizens with an active interest in the empire, these legionnaires had a tangible stake in its power and property. They tended to regard the empire's enemies as outlaws and criminals, and treated them with predictable harshness. The war historian Lynn Montross noted that the typical Roman soldier "displayed few of those whims of mercy or generosity which varied the routine cruelties of other ancient warriors."[3]

Because they must be free to move frequently and quickly from one frontier to another, legionnaires were forbidden to marry. They accommodated nature by keeping women in the civilian quarters that grew up around their barracks.

Roman officials allowed the Jewish political and religious establishment to direct the day-to-day lives of the people. The highest Jewish authority was the Sanhedrin, a council of 71 members, most of them from the wealthy, aristocratic Sadducees party. The high priest of the year was its convenor and president. Technically, the Sanhedrin had jurisdiction over all religious and legal matters, except for political offenses, understood by the Romans as anything that constituted a threat to their rule.

Most people in Judea and Galilee went about their business, ignoring the Roman presence as much as they could. Like occupied people everywhere, they tried to avoid being squeezed too tightly by their conquerers. Many came to terms with these foreigners in the way conquered people have done throughout history: don't bother them and they won't bother you.

Resistance: Violent and Nonviolent

But revolution was in the air.

When a group of daring men under the leadership of Judas of Galilee, founder of the Zealots, raided a Roman arms supply depot in Sepphoris, the Romans rounded up 2,000 suspected revolutionaries and crucified them along the road between Sepphoris and Nazareth, 6 miles away. This happened in the year A.D. 6, when Jesus was about 10 years old. He may well have seen the crosses.[4]

The Zealots were a group of Pharisees, strict observers of the law, who had separated themselves from the mainstream of society and, because of their zeal to see the law practiced without outside interference, refused to obey the Romans. They were not willing to wait patiently for a future Messiah, but wanted to become actively involved in the messianic transformation of their people by driving the Romans out.

No match for the overwhelming military superiority of the Romans, they established hiding places in the nearly inaccessible eastern slopes of the hill country of Judea. From there they could make lightning strikes on the occupying forces. The Romans looked on them as robbers and bandits. The priests, the Sadducees, and other Pharisees considered them dangerous disturbers of the peace. In the eyes of most of the people, they were heroes.

At least one of Jesus' closest disciples, Simon, was a Zealot.

Not all the resistance to the Romans was violent. The Jewish historian Josephus has given details of one action which, apparently spontaneously, used nonviolent tactics to persuade the Roman governor, Pilate, to remove pictures of Caesar from the Temple in Jerusalem. Any image, but especially of the Roman emperor who was considered a god by many of his subjects, seriously violated Jewish sensitivities.

When the pictures were first discovered in the Temple (Pilate had ordered them put in at night) a large crowd of people, "multitudes," Josephus said, assembled before Pilate's headquarters in Caesarea on the Mediterranean coast, 60 miles northwest of Jerusalem. For 5 days and nights they demonstrated publicly, demanding that Pilate remove the offensive images.

At first he would not even talk to the demonstrators. Then he decided to drive them away by force. Ordering his soldiers to surround the crowd, Pilate went out into the square to address the protestors. He told them that unless they ceased immediately and dispersed they would all be killed. Josephus described what happened:

> They threw themselves on the ground and laid their necks bare and said they would take their death very willingly rather than that the wisdom of their law should be transgressed. Upon which Pilate was deeply affected with their firm resolution to keep their laws inviolable, and presently commanded the images to be carried back to Caesarea.[5]

Their willingness to suffer even death from the legionnaires' swords moved Pilate to give in to their demand and remove the offensive images from the Temple.

This incident, as far as can be determined, occurred in A.D. 26, the year that Jesus probably began his public ministry.

The Kingdom of God

The gospels do not portray Jesus as a Zealot, eager for the violent overthrow of Roman occupation. Nor do they portray him as a nonviolent political activist. The revolutionary character of his life lay in the ideas he promulgated and in his own personal stance toward the society of his time.

The main theme of his teaching, according to the first three gospels, was that the kingdom of God was at hand. Mark summarized it: "Jesus went into Galilee, proclaiming the good news of God. 'The time has come,' he said. 'The kingdom of God is near. Repent and believe the good news' " (Mark 1:14-15).[6]

The kingdom of God was a familiar image to his listeners. Many of them had a vivid picture of what it was to be like when God finally fulfilled his promises and established his kingdom on earth. It was to be a kingdom of peace, where the lion would lie down with the lamb, and where all nations would worship the true God. They, the chosen people, would be at the center of the kingdom, receiving the choicest blessings, respected and admired by all. The hated Romans would no longer be a problem.

This great earthly panorama, in which the splendors of heaven would be mirrored in the joy and blessedness of all creation in final harmony, would be brought about through the instrumentality of a special envoy sent by God, his anointed one, the Messiah.

Now Jesus was preaching that the kingdom was near. But none of the expected characteristics was in evidence.

Instead, Jesus indicated that the kingdom was looking quite different. When John the Baptist sent his followers to inquire if Jesus was the expected Messiah, the signs they had anticipated were not present. Instead, the kingdom with which Jesus was involved had different characteristics. "Go back and report to John what you hear and see: the blind receive sight, the lame walk, those who have leprosy are cured, the deaf hear, the dead are raised, and the good news is preached to the poor" (Mt. 11:4-5).

Earlier, Jesus had preached in a synagogue in his hometown of Nazareth that he was involved in fulfilling the messianic prophecy of Isaiah: "The Spirit of the Lord is on me, because he has anointed me to preach good news to the poor. He has sent me to proclaim freedom for the prisoners and recovery of sight for the blind, to release the oppressed" (Lk. 4:18).

Those who would be specially blessed in this new kingdom would be the poor in spirit, those who mourn, the meek, those who hunger and thirst for righteousness, the merciful, the pure in heart, the peacemakers, people persecuted because of righteousness (Mt. 5:3-10).

Those who would receive the most attention and the most concern would be the blind, the lame, the sick, the deaf, the handicapped, the prisoners, the oppressed, anyone in need of healing and liberation.

This was an entirely different kind of kingdom than most people expected. It called for a change of attitude. "Repent," Jesus said. Change your way of thinking, your way of living. This kingdom is turning your normal value system upside down. And, then, "Believe." Open yourself to this new reality that God is bringing to pass now. It really is good news.

It is good news especially to those on the bottom of society, rejected because they are poor, so poor that even their hearts, their souls, their spirits, feel poor. The poor are the first ones Jesus identifies as being involved in the kingdom. "Blessed are you who are poor, for yours is the Kingdom of God" (Lk 6:20).

To be a part of this kingdom people should love God above all, Jesus taught. But they should also love their neighbors with the same directness and concern they show to God. The neighbor, he explained by the parable of the Good Samaritan (Lk 10:25-37), is anyone in need. Helping that neighbor is so important that eternal salvation depends on it, he implied by the vision of the sheep and the goats separated at the Last Judgment (Mt 25:31-46).

To prove that a person really does have love of neighbor, one should love the most difficult neighbors of all, one's enemies (Mt. 5:44).

At those moments when life is divided between the oppressors and the oppressed, members of the kingdom will be on the side of the oppressed. Sometimes this means angering the oppressors. But the call is clear. "Blessed are those who hunger and thirst for righteousness" (Mt 5:6).

Rejecting the socially esteemed values of wealth, success, and personal acclaim, Jesus taught generosity, giving, self-restraint, simplicity, and humility. Don't worry so much, he said. This is God's kingdom. This is really the way he wants you to live.

The Dangerous Jesus

If his teaching ran counter to the prevailing climate of opinion, so did his actions. Jesus was a friend of outcasts, criminals, prostitutes, and, above all, the poor, with whom he spent most of his time. He did not have a steady job, did not settle down, get married, and raise a family. He repudiated wealth, and consistently refused to provide for his own security. His life, like his teachings, ran counter to many culturally accepted attitudes.[7] But they got right to the heart of what the kingdom of heaven was all about.

Social relationships, according to him, should be based on service and humility, not authority and subservience. The society of his time involved domination and exploitation, maintained by violence. Jesus rejected domination. After describing the way Gentile kings, like the Romans, lord it over their subjects, he said to his followers, "But you are not to be like that. Instead, the greatest among you should be like the youngest, and the one who rules like the one who serves" (Lk 22:26).

Because the Pharisees were laying heavy burdens on people, imposing a kind of religious captivity, Jesus confronted them. "Woe to you, teachers of the law and Pharisees, you hypocrites! You give a tenth of your spices — mint, dill and cummin. But you have neglected the more important matters of the law — justice, mercy and faithfulness" (Mt 23:23). "You snakes!" he called them. "You brood of vipers! How will you escape being condemned to hell?" (Mt 23:33).

This was no meek and mild Jesus, silently suffering the

abuses of the leaders of his people. He stood up to them. He confronted them publicly, courageously, and nonviolently.

And they were threatened by him. If Jesus' teaching and example spread, if large numbers of people began to live in the way he was calling for, their society would change significantly. In the new society everyone would be fundamentally equal. No one would be pushed aside because of poverty or sickness or old age. Sharing and caring would be the outstanding features.

As this new community developed, the structured society of the day would crumble. The point was not lost on the leaders of that society. Jesus was threatening their power and their place in a more decisive way than the Roman overlords, with whom they had already reached an accommodation.

He was even more dangerous than the armed rebels in the hills. Even if the Zealots had been successful and the Romans driven out, the Jewish power structure would have continued. But if Jesus' way had come to prevail, that structure would be thoroughly undermined. Jesus was doing what no political leaders can long tolerate. He was infecting the people with ideas that ran contrary to the patterns assuring their leadership. If enough people no longer believe in, want, or will tolerate those patterns, the whole thing begins to come apart.

If the danger was not apparent in rural Galilee, it was clear in Jerusalem. Jesus had to be stopped. He was a danger to the nation, as they understood the nation.

Jesus was perceived as inciting unrest, creating a climate of resistance to established authority. If it went much further, the immediate danger was that the Romans would not tolerate it, and would indiscriminately crush the Jewish society that operated at their pleasure.

The decision to have Jesus eliminated was taken in a national security context. The gospel of John describes it:

> Then the chief priests and the Pharisees called a meeting of the Sanhedrin. "What are we accomplishing?" they asked. "Here is this man performing many miraculous signs. If we let him go on like this, everyone will believe in him, and then the

Romans will come and take away both our place and our nation." Then one of them, named Caiaphas, who was high priest that year, spoke up, "You know nothing at all! You do not realize that it is better for you that one man die for the people than that the whole nation perish." . . . So from that day on they plotted to take his life (Jn 11:47-50, 53).

The charge before Pilate, from whom the leaders of the Sanhedrin were asking the death penalty, was sedition.

And they began to accuse him, saying, "We have found this man subverting our nation. He opposes payment of taxes to Caesar and claims to be Christ, a king. . . . He stirs up the people all over Judea by his teaching. He started in Galilee and has come all the way here" (Lk 23:2,5).

And so he was executed. The dreaded Roman crunch was deferred.

It finally came in the year 70, when four Roman legions, twenty thousand veteran troops under a general named Titus, crushed an outbreak of violence, captured Jerusalem, and burned down the Temple. Three years later, when the last fortress of Masada on the Dead Sea was overcome and its defenders killed themselves, all resistance ended.

The conquerers carried the seven-branched candlestick from the Temple back to Rome in triumph, an event depicted vividly on the memorial arch erected there to Titus. The image in the stone can be seen in Rome today.

The nation whose security its leaders had been so concerned to preserve was destroyed, and its people were scattered.

The Peaceful Jesus

But the ideas Jesus taught survived. And they spread, more widely and more rapidly, through the power of his resurrection, than anyone dared hope before his death.

Nothing in these ideas, nothing in his life, favored war or killing. Jesus in an army uniform, as he was pictured during World War I, or wearing a guerrilla cartridge belt, as a poster in the 1960's showed him, can only be imagined by superimposing these military

patterns on the Jesus of the gospels. Nothing in his life or teachings as proclaimed in the New Testament supports these interpretations.

Efforts have been made by those who justify war to find support for their position in the New Testament. They point to Jesus' driving the money changers from the Temple as a time when he used violence.

Although this event is mentioned in all four gospels, only that of John includes the detail that Jesus used a whip. The other gospels suggest that Jesus acted assertively and with passion, but give no indication that he did bodily harm to anyone. In John's gospel the original Greek text indicates that Jesus used a whip to drive out the animals. It is not at all clear that he used it on the money changers. This more accurate reading is reflected in contemporary English translations of the New Testament.

The passage in the New International Version, for example, reads:

> When it was almost time for the Jewish Passover, Jesus went up to Jerusalem. In the temple courts he found men selling cattle, sheep and doves, and others sitting at tables exchanging money. So he made a whip out of cords, and drove all from the temple area, both sheep and cattle; he scattered the coins of the money changers and overturned their tables. To those who sold doves he said, "Get these out of here! How dare you turn my Father's house into a market!" (Jn 2:13-16).

The belief that Jesus whipped human beings in the Temple on that one occasion is based on an inaccurate translation. But in any event, as historian Roland Bainton has remarked, "the whip of cords, if genuine, was no hand grenade." One cannot validly deduce the legitimacy of war from Jesus' action against the money changers.

Another text often cited in support of war contains Jesus' advice to "Give to Caesar what is Caesar's, and to God what is God's" (Mt 22:21; Mk 12:17; Lk 20:25). When Caesar calls for military service in defense of the nation, it should be given to him, according to this view.

Jesus' words must first be understood in the context in which they were spoken. He was asked whether it was lawful to pay taxes to the Roman emperor. The question, posed by some Pharisees and Herodians, was designed to trap him. If he said yes, he could be accused of giving support to the hated conquerors. If he said no, he could be turned over to the Roman authorities as advocating rebellion.

Jesus did not reply right away. He asked his questioners to show him a coin, the kind that would be used to pay the taxes. They produced a denarius, on which was engraved a picture of Caesar. Immediately they stood revealed as lax observers of the Jewish law, which prohibited any kind of images. The fact that they were carrying these coins put them in violation of Jewish law. Jesus' answer to them was: as long as you are willing to compromise yourself by using Caesar's money, you should give him what he demands. Then he quickly added something that had not been mentioned previously in the conversation. But give "to God what is God's."

When God calls for something, he should be obeyed. When God calls for something that goes contrary to what Caesar demands, it is clear whose law takes precedence. If Caesar demands military training, preparedness to kill, and in fact orders his troops to commit mass murder, one who is aware of God's demands to preserve life knows that this command of Caesar must not be obeyed.

Paul's Version

The overall picture of Jesus' teaching was clear. Not only is it wrong to kill, it is even wrong to hate an enemy. No one should be the object of retaliation. If a person is struck in the face, the other side of the face must be offered also. Warmakers are not blessed, peacemakers are.

The lifestyle Jesus advocated was spelled out further by Paul:

Bless those who persecute you; bless and do not curse. Rejoice with those who rejoice; mourn with those who mourn. Live in harmony with one another. Do not be proud, but be willing to associate with people of low position. Do not be conceited. Do not repay anyone evil for evil. Be careful to do what is right in the eyes of everybody. If it is possible, as far as it depends on you, live at peace with everyone. Do not take revenge, my friends, but leave room for God's wrath, for it is written, "It is mine to avenge; I will repay," says the Lord.

Paul concludes, quoting from the book of Proverbs:

On the contrary: "If your enemy is hungry, feed him; if he is thirsty, give him something to drink. In doing this, you will heap burning coals on his head." Do not be overcome by evil, but overcome evil with good (Rom. 12:14-21).

This superb summation, which has been called the great pacifist paragraph of the New Testament, shows how a Christian should approach all enemies, personal as well as national. Paul follows these words with some advice which, like Jesus' observation about giving to Caesar, are sometimes used to support going to war when the government deems it necessary.

Everyone must submit himself to the governing authorities, for there is no authority except that which God has established. The authorities that exist have been established by God. Consequently, he who rebels against the authority is rebelling against what God has instituted, and those who do so will bring judgment on themselves (Rom. 13:1-2).

Paul would not be likely to contradict what he had written immediately before, so he cannot be referring to war and military service when he encourages obedience to the governing authorities. Paul's thinking was that civil laws, where they do not contradict the law of God, are necessary to regulate human interchanges, and should normally be obeyed.[8]

Those who see in this text a duty to submit to military service, and kill if the government commands it, are wrenching it from its New Testament context.

Those who support the morality of war can find little comfort in the New Testament.

The God of War

But the Old Testament gives them plenty of comfort. God is portrayed as the Lord of hosts, leading his people in war. The land he promised them was won through war. The Temple he ordered built was to be in a city that had to be captured by war. His chosen people had to fight against powerful and hostile neighbors. Sometimes God ordered them to kill everyone on the enemy side after a battle, including women and children.

The theologians who later developed the just war tradition supported their theories with citations from the Old, not the New, Testament.

The fundamental Christian principle for interpreting the Old Testament is to look at it in light of the New. Jesus showed the way when he gave new meaning to some of the writings of the law and the prophets. "You have heard that it was said to the people long ago, 'Do not murder, and anyone who murders will be subject to judgment.' But I tell you that anyone who is angry with his brother will be subject to judgment" (Mt 5:21-2).

The events and even the commandments in the Old Testament are to be viewed from the perspective of the life and teachings of Jesus. If the Old Testament God was portrayed as sanctioning war, after Jesus he can no longer be understood to do so. Some scholars striving to find continuity and consistency between the two Testaments say that perhaps God had special reasons for encouraging the wars of his chosen people. He wanted to teach them of his power and might, perhaps. Through him, rather than on their own, they were able to defeat enemies stronger than themselves.

He led them in their struggle for survival in the face of threats of annihilation. He wanted them to have the land and prosper in it. He wanted to preserve them so that through them his ways would be made known to the whole world. From them he would bring forth the Messiah, the savior of the world. Once the savior came there was no longer need for these wars. Now God could teach the fullness of his designs for his human creatures. These designs do not include war. So runs a typical Christian theological interpretation.

Peace eyes bring an additional insight into the wars of the Old Testament. They see the Old Testament as a marvelous collection of writings produced by a remarkable people over a thousand years. This people was convinced that the one true God had singled them out, that he was their God, no one else's, and that they alone were his people.

In their conflicts they assumed he was on their side. Their enemies were his enemies. "Whenever the Ark set out, Moses said, 'Rise up, O Lord, may your enemies be scattered; may your foes flee before you' " (Num. 10:35).

Because their enemies are also God's, he should be called on for help in the approaching battle.

O God, do not keep silent; be not quiet, O God, be not still. See how your enemies are astir, how your foes rear their heads . . . Make them like tumbleweed, O my God, like chaff before the wind. As fire consumes the forest, or a flame sets the mountains ablaze, so pursue them with your tempest and terrify them with your storm (Ps. 83:1-2, 13-15).

When God is portrayed as answering these prayers, he is also seen as ordering the excesses that occurred after the victory.

This is what the Lord Almighty says: "I will punish the Amalekites for what they did to Israel when they waylaid them as they came up from Egypt. Now go, attack the Amalekites and totally destroy everything that belongs to them. Do not spare them; put to death men and women, children and infants, cattle and sheep, camels and donkeys" (I Sam. 15:2-3).

In this understanding of God, the people of the tribes of Israel were no different from tribal people in other parts of the world. An Osage Indian, as he set off on a raiding expedition, prayed to his god: "Pity me, Wohkonda! I am very poor. Give me success against my enemies. Let me avenge the death of my friends. Let me take many scalps, many horses."[9]

This Nootka Indian prayer was said when embarking on an attack: "Great Quahootze! Let me live, not be sick, find the enemy, not be afraid of him, find him asleep, and kill many of him."

On one of the South Pacific islands there was a special prayer for the beginning of a thieving expedition:

O thou divine Outre-reter! We go out for plunder. Cause all
things to sleep in the house. Owner of the house, sleep on!
Threshold of the house, sleep on! Little insects of the house,
sleep on! Central post, rafters, thatch of the house, sleep on!
O Rongo, grant us success!

Tribal people assumed that their gods were concerned with
only their tribe. If they won a conflict with another tribe, it proved
their superiority and the superiority of their god. They had no con-
ception of a deity that might have a concern for them and also for
the people they were about to attack and plunder.

The legitimacy of war today should find no more support
from the Old Testament than the legitimacy of slavery, polygamy,
and killing witches. All of these culturally accepted practices were
enshrined in the Hebrew Scriptures.

Shalom

The Old Testament, though, does present an attractive vision of peace.

The Psalmist understood God's message this way: "I will listen to what God the Lord will say; he promises peace to his people,
his saints" (Ps. 85:8). Not only for his people and his saints, but for
everyone will God do away with war. "He makes wars to cease to
the ends of the earth; he breaks the bow and shatters the spear, he
burns the shields with fire" (Ps. 46:9). The prophets see in the last
days, when God's rule is established, "they will beat their swords
into plowshares, their spears into pruning hooks. Nation will not
take up sword against nation, nor will they train for war anymore"
(Is. 2:4, Mic. 4:3).

The Hebrew Scriptures are a rich source for understanding
the fundamental human desire in every age and culture for an end
to war and the dawn of the day of peace, when nations would live
together in the fullness of their shared humanity.

The vision of peace derived from the bible is much richer
than the negative concept of the cessation of war. It is a positive
condition of well-being in which people live in harmony with each
other and with God.

Strength in Persecution

The 20th century has witnessed an unparalleled parade of totalitarian regimes that have abused their peoples in horrible ways. Summary and brutal arrests, long and sordid imprisonments, cruel and degrading tortures, mass executions without trial, these have become sadly familiar patterns perpetrated by governments trying to whip their people into line to maintain the kind of order necessary for the regime's prosperity. The repressive actions are directed against suspected subversives, those who, because they think or act differently, threaten the stranglehold of power exercised by the few at the top.

Toward the end of the New Testament era the Roman empire was acting this way. Its litmus test of loyalty was the worship of its gods. Suspected subversives were rounded up, put to the test, and if they refused to worship were tortured, and executed, often for the public amusement of safe Romans.

As Christianity spread around the Mediterranean world during the half century following Jesus' death, Christians were often targeted for the test. They were suspect because they worshipped a different God.

The emperor Domition in the last decade of the first century decreed that he himself was "dominus et deus," lord and god, and that all the world must worship him. Christians refused. Many of them were rounded up, tortured, and if they persisted in their refusal, killed in the brutal fashion of the time.

The book of Revelation, placed at the end of the New Testament, was written during these times. Although it has been interpreted in different ways over the past 19 centuries, often as prophecy about future events, especially about the end of the world, its principal purpose was to encourage Christians to remain faithful in that trying time of Domition's persecution.

Using imagery only thinly veiled, its author, John, described Rome as the new Babylon, the new power threatening captivity for God's people. It is the great prostitute sitting on "seven hills" (17:9), "drunk with the blood of the saints, the blood of those who bore testimony to Jesus" (17:6). To make sure his readers got the point,

John added, "The woman you saw is the great city that rules over the kings of the earth" (17:18). He said that Rome is in the service of the great red dragon in the heavens, the force of evil.

Many will be killed during this harsh time, but they will find their glory before the throne of God.

> I looked and there before me was a great multitude that no one could count, from every nation, tribe, people and language, standing before the throne and in front of the Lamb. They were wearing white robes and were holding palm branches in their hands. . . . These are they who have come out of the great tribulation; they have washed their robes and made them white in the blood of the Lamb (7:9,14).

It is important to remain steadfast, because the justice of God will eventually triumph. In "the new Jerusalem, coming down out of heaven . . . God himself will be with them and be their God. He will wipe every tear from their eyes. There will be no more death or mourning or crying or pain, for the old order of things has passed away" (21:1,3-4).

Those who stand strong, even if they are killed, will reap the rewards of their courage for Christ. "Blessed are those who wash their robes, that they may have the right to the tree of life and may go through the gates into the city" (22:14).

Before the first century had ended, Jesus' followers were facing the same question he had been asked in another context. Is it lawful to give tribute to Caesar? As the book of Revelation entered Christian consciousness in A.D. 95, Caesar was seen as the head of a murderous empire that dominated the world and coerced people to submit to it. The author of Revelation felt that the only adequate Christian response was a firm withdrawal from the ways of Rome.

Many believers today see a similar need to withdraw from the ways of the world's contemporary Romes, but at the same time defend the values of justice and freedom. They find considerable help in the nonviolent techniques developed in the 20th century.

4   THE DYNAMICS OF NONVIOLENCE

Nonviolence is the greatest force at the disposal of mankind. It is mightier than the mightiest weapon of destruction devised by the ingenuity of man.

—Mahatma Gandhi

Rejecting the murderous plans of today's Caesars is only the beginning. One must say no when assessing nuclear idols in the light of Judaeo-Christian faith. It is a no not only to the actual use of nuclear weapons, but also to the threat of using them. It is therefore a

67

no to the deployment, production, and planning of the weapons, and to a nation's foreign and domestic policies based on them.

But negativity alone is a poor basis for life. It is injurious to psychological health, it induces bitterness, and is remarkably unattractive. The positive peace proclaimed in the bible as shalom or the kingdom of God calls for direct action. The action that is demanded is not random or frantic, but faith-based and purposeful. Its criterion is always love of neighbor, both the nearest neighbor and the most distant neighbor who may be indirectly affected.

Action for peace will be, if at all possible, nonviolent.

If nuclear weapons are the final step on the ladder of violence, rejecting them propels a person toward the ladder of nonviolence. The first rung on this ladder is to begin thinking how conflicts can be resolved without recourse to violence.

Conflicts are bound to occur when human beings, or nations, interact. The only way to avoid conflict is to avoid interaction. That may be possible for those who can escape to a desert island or a mountain retreat. It may have been possible in times past for nations who were economically self-sufficient and isolated by impregnable natural borders, but no nation in the 20th century can avoid interaction.

Distances have been closed through jet travel and electronic communication. Economic needs make interrelations an inevitable feature of international life. No nation in the 20th century can avoid international conflicts.

When a nation finds itself involved in a conflict it has three recourses. It can (1) capitulate, surrender, give in, allow itself to be dominated; (2) engage with force, perhaps leading to violence, in an effort to win or at least stop the conflict; or (3) engage nonviolently.

The first response, passive acquiescence out of weakness, fear or distaste for difficult situations, creates a false peace. Domination of one party by another leads to resentment, hostility, and often to an outbreak of resistance that raises the conflict to a higher level.

The second way, force, may bring on war. Policy makers

frequently take this risk, following the conventional wisdom summarized by Mao Zedong: "War can only be abolished through war, and in order to get rid of the gun it is necessary to take up the gun."

The third way, nonviolence, involves a whole range of other possibilities. Some of these techniques are readily available. All nations maintain diplomatic corps. They frequently engage in conferences, negotiations, and treaties. Many seek to resolve differences by bargaining, or by third-party arbitration. All of these are nonviolent means.

But should these fail and the conflict intensify, there is another kind of nonviolent action that can bring about a radical solution and lead to a firm and realistic peace. It was brought to the world's attention by Mohandas Gandhi, the Mahatma (Great-souled One), in the liberation of India.

Truth Force

The word nonviolence came into the English language from the Sanscrit word ahimsa, meaning non-harm, long a principle in the religions of Hinduism, Buddhism, and Jainism. It was the basis of Gandhi's campaigns. Gandhi's first principle was to avoid harming his opponents.[1]

His motivating energy was a deep inner conviction, which he called satyagraha, truth force, the power of truth. For Gandhi, truth was God, and Gandhi believed his work for the liberation of his people was in harmony with God. Love of all living creatures was his ideal, including the hardest love of all, of his enemies.

Gandhi understood that an oppressor is carrying a heavy weight. Not only do victims of injustice suffer, but the perpetrators also are weighed down by having to maintain a distorted life. Gandhi wanted to free his Indian people from British rule, but he also wanted to free the British from their burden of colonialism.

Nonviolence, as Gandhi understood it, is positive action for true human good, motivated by love, using only means that help and do not harm.

A typical conflict involves two parties, each of whom wants to prevail. Gandhian nonviolence begins with the assumption that prevailing or winning is not the proper goal; it seeks to work out the truth of the situation.

Gandhi's conflict involved the British government's colonial rule over India and the struggle of the Indian people to free themselves from that domination. Truth, Gandhi believed, required that the Indian people govern themselves. The British must withdraw. They should leave not because they were defeated, but because they became convinced of the truth of the matter. That is, in fact, what eventually happened in 1947, after thirty years of conflict.

Abraham Lincoln once remarked, "I destroy my enemies when I make them my friends." Gandhi said his own greatest achievement was that the British withdrew from India not as defeated enemies, but as new friends.

The Way It Works

To communicate the truth takes courage, courage to stand up and tell an aggressor that what is happening is wrong, and say it repeatedly and in many ways.

The aggressor's first reaction is the normal human defense mechanism. "I'm not an aggressor. You're wrong. Keep quiet." And then, "If you don't keep quiet I'll beat you." And, "If you still don't keep quiet I'll put you in prison or I'll kill you."

The truth of the matter is rarely immediately apparent to the aggressor. That it ever does become apparent, that a new attitude does develop, is the result of the dynamics of nonviolence.

The most critical assumption underlying all nonviolent action is that both parties in the conflict share a common humanity. However much it may be obscured at times all people, even professional torturers and battle-scarred militarists, have a deep-seated tendency toward love and justice. Their humanity may be distorted by ideology, warped by a desire for power, temporarily buried under the weight of official duties, obscured by habits of violence, but it is always there.[2]

Except in times of total insanity, when everything essentially human is inoperable, the person who is mentally and emotionally active has an inherent affinity for truth and love.

Nonviolence works by appealing to this essential humanity in the adversary. At some point nonviolent action, in courage and love, can trigger a reciprocal response in the opponent, can fan the spark of human decency which, no matter how low it may burn in an individual for a time, cannot be extinguished completely.[3]

The key to triggering this humane response is the nonviolent activist's courageous willingness to suffer for what is right and just and true. If the aggressor meets violence, continued aggression becomes self-justifying. But it is difficult to sustain aggression against someone who is not fighting back, someone who is courageously and lovingly facing the attacker, preferring to suffer rather than enter into the chain of violence.

The nonviolent person does not act like a victim, bowing down and passively accepting blows and assaults. The recognition of common humanity occurs when the would-be victim stands strong in the courage of conviction, and is willing to take the blows in order to witness to the truth. If the aggressor begins to recognize in the sufferer the humanity they have in common, the aggression falters.

The goal of nonviolent action is not to repress or defeat, but to convert, to allow the person who is enemy to live according to the better part of human nature rather than by the violence that has been dominant. When the change takes place the person is no longer an enemy who must be overcome, but a cooperator in finding a peaceful solution.

Critics of nonviolence say that Gandhi's success was due to the fact that his opponent, Great Britain, was at heart a Christian country. Its soldiers were decent and humane, and when they were faced with masses of people willing to suffer for their beliefs, they granted independence rather than attack these people. Their motives, it is alleged, were humanitarian.

The same condition, they suggest, accounted for the relative gains made by Martin Luther King and the civil rights movement in the United States. If King or Gandhi had spoken out as they had in Nazi Germany or Stalinist Russia or Garcia's El Salvador, they would immediately have been arrested and simply disappeared.

The objection ignores two historical facts. The first is that the actions of the British soldiers, and their Indian subordinates, were anything but humane and Christian. The soldiers and police beat Gandhi's protestors with batons and rifle butts. They fired into crowds and clubbed demonstrators until they were exhausted by the effort to swing the clubs. They arrested Gandhi many times. If he had disappeared others would have stepped forward to take his place, such was the strength of the movement he inspired.

The second fact is the real success that nonviolent resistance has had in countries under brutal regimes. Organized nonviolent actions in Norway, Denmark, France, and the Netherlands time and again brought about changes during the Nazi occupation.

Nonviolence can work even in the face of the bitter racial hostility and terrorism, such as that in present-day South Africa and the southern United States in the 1960's. It may not be efficacious all the time or in every situation, but a strong case can be made that it has more of a chance of being successful, and with less loss of life, than organized violence. And it lacks the dangers of escalation inherent in a violent response to oppression.

The process by which success is won demands courage, inner strength, and concerted activity. It is in no way identified with the cowardice or passivity often associated with the word nonviolence by those who have only a hazy understanding of it. King used the phrase "nonviolent direct action" to refer to the whole array of efforts in which his people were involved in their campaign for civil rights.

The nonviolent activist must be ready to suffer. Besides courage and a clear mind, he or she must have the self-denial that is ready to face sacrifice. Active nonviolence is not easy. Where there is injustice, this must be righted. Where there is oppression, there must be freedom. This calls for knowledge of technique, and coordinated, persevering activity.

Kinds of Nonviolent Action

Peace researcher Gene Sharp has identified 198 different actions that can be called nonviolent and used to resisting aggression.[4] He grouped these into three principal categories:

1. *Protest and Persuasion.* This includes any show of disapproval of a course of events, from telling a person that what he or she is doing should be stopped, to letter-writing campaigns, petitions, vigils, marches, and rallies. The purpose is to bring a conflict to light, expose it, in the hopes that those responsible for the injustice will see the truth and change things.

If the social climate is tolerant, these methods are relatively easy to carry out. But when the views expressed are unpopular, or go against government policy, then even the mildest action may require great courage and can have a significant impact.

2. *Noncooperation.* Refusal to allow some functions of a society to operate, through a strike or boycott, is a second level of nonviolent action. In the face of injustice people may choose to stop assisting certain activities. Refusing to pay taxes, resisting the draft, rejecting unjust laws (called civil disobedience), closing down places of business, these kinds of noncooperation can impede or even halt the normal functioning of a society.

All these initiatives carry the risk of personal loss or injury. Willingness to accept the loss or suffer the injury is a key element in their effectiveness.

3. *Intervention.* A significant step beyond withdrawing cooperation is taken when people directly insert themselves into a social process in a way that brings it to a temporary halt. Occupying buildings, holding sit-ins, blocking entrances, standing across a roadway, lying down on railroad tracks, all these actions confront authorities with persons putting themselves in vulnerable positions in an effort to stop important activities. The purpose is to draw attention to specific operations that are part of the unjust system, and to show the oppressor the strength of the resistance movement.

Intervention poses a more direct and immediate challenge to the status quo. It leads to quicker success or to sharper repression for a while, as the dynamics of nonviolence continue working for a constructive change.

Seeking Truth

Gandhi's insistence that nonviolence be based on truth raises important questions. How can one be sure that one's cause is, in fact, true? Can't there be truth on both sides? Isn't it insufferably arrogant to claim that my way and only my way is true? More than arrogance, doesn't insistence on truth lead to intolerance and fanaticism? Gandhi thought so. He said:

> I am but a seeker after Truth. I claim to have found a way to it. I claim to be making a ceaseless effort to find it. But I admit that I have not yet found it. To find Truth completely is to realize oneself and one's destiny, that is, to become perfect. I am painfully conscious of my imperfections.[5]

The nonviolent activist, believing that he or she cannot know truth absolutely enough to take human life in its name, resorts to means that respect human dignity, not destroy it. Gandhi said that satyagraha excludes the use of violence because human beings are "not capable of knowing the absolute truth and, therefore, not competent to punish."

Anyone probing for truth must approach the quest with humility, open to the insights of others, always ready to adjust one's perceptions with new knowledge or different perspectives. But the difficulties in achieving truth need not be paralyzing. There are some situations in which truth is clearly evident: slavery, child-abuse, torture, concentration camps.

Truth must be sought carefully and resolutely in other, less obvious, conflicts, Aware of personal tendencies toward self-righteousness, the truth seeker must be ready to accept honest criticism and change direction if a better way becomes evident. Until that happens, the part of the truth one has discovered will continue to guide the way.

The truth about war leads the person concerned for a nonviolent alternative to look carefully at what is going on inside a country as well as at threats from outside.

Clausewitz's classical description of war as "a continuation of political relations, a carrying out of the same by other means"[6] is accepted as accurate by most analysts. This implies that war is an extension first of a country's peacetime policies toward other nations, and secondly its economic and social policies toward its own citizens. If these policies involve exploitation and injustice, a realistic alternative to war must include efforts to transform them, because they are the seeds of war.

Nonviolence in Action

The 20th century has witnessed hundreds of nonviolent campaigns for human dignity and liberation. They have had varying degrees of success.

Martin Luther King translated Gandhi's satyagraha as soul force. He adapted Gandhi's tactics of marches, boycotts, and civil disobedience — nonviolent direct action — to the campaign for the civil rights of black Americans in the southern United States. King wanted all participants in his activities to agree to follow the principles of nonviolence.

Danilo Dolci engaged in a persevering nonviolent campaign in Sicily against the power of the Mafia.

Archbishop Helder Camara helped his people in the northeast area of Brazil organize nonviolent campaigns for decent food, housing, and education despite the structural violence that plagues his country.

Since the early 1970's, a group of farmers in the Larzac region of southern France has successfully resisted the government's efforts to take their fields to enlarge a nearby military base.

Tens of thousands of poor farmworkers in the United States, in explicitly nonviolent campaigns under the leadership of Caesar Chavez, obtained basic labor rights in the face of political and economic discrimination.

Dorothy Day in New York City motivated several generations of Catholic workers to provide direct assistance to the poorest of the poor, and to resist nonviolently those laws of her country that promote militarism.

Some campaigns, like the women's rights struggle and the labor movement, have used predominantly nonviolent tactics for worthy goals without explicitly affirming their nonviolent character.

Many struggles, although nonviolent for the most part, have included some violence, like the movement to stop the Vietnam War and the struggle against apartheid in South Africa.

The resistance of the Polish people in early 1982 was at first largely nonviolent. Martial law was met by workers shutting down shipyards and factories, by miners stopping coal production, by farmers withholding produce from markets, and by thousands of determined men and women demonstrating in the streets.

Civilian-Based Defense

The Polish resistance demonstrated a fundamental principle underlying nonviolence: government is effective only with the consent of the governed. If the people refuse to cooperate, if they courageously stand up to intimidation, the economic and political system of a country will not work.

Bayonets cannot bake bread; guns cannot produce butter. Tanks can crush, but they cannot construct.

Peace researchers, particularly in Europe, have outlined a program involving active resistance to aggression. The resistance does not rely on military force, but on large numbers of trained, disciplined civilians.

The effectiveness of this kind of defense is illustrated in the hypothetical case of a country which, when threatened by potential enemies, would make a deliberate decision to adopt an active resistance policy instead of relying on its armed forces. The country would announce to the world that it is getting rid of its tanks, planes, warships, bombs, and shells. It would terminate all defense treaties with militarily powerful nations, and would not invite them to intervene on its behalf.

This announcement itself would shift world opinion to the side of the disarmed nation. Aggressive action against the nation would go against the tide of this opinion.

Before the public announcement, the country would have ready a trained corps of nonviolent professionals prepared to take leadership roles in a national emergency. Not every citizen would have undergone the training. But, through ordinary channels of education and communication, all would know about it and know what was expected of them should their national security be threatened.

It would be no more necessary that every person be fully disciplined for nonviolence, than that every citizen in a nation preparing for war be fully disciplined for combat. But all would understand the idea of nonviolence, know that they should cooperate with the trained officers, and be disciplined enough to do nothing through anger, or through personal or group violence to interfere with national operations.

The constant aim of this defense is to make it impossible for an outside force to establish and maintain power over the country. It is based on the theory that political power ultimately depends on acceptance by the people. Force and fear can work to a certain extent, but finally no individual or group can govern without the consent of the society.

Nonviolent civilian defense could not stop an aggressor's bombs or tanks, nor could it prevent an invasion. But it could make the invasion eventually worthless, because the invaded society would not produce goods, yield its resources, or submit to the aggressor's will.

The landing force would be met by refusal to accept its legitimacy. Citizens would reject orders to operate the machinery of the country. The transportation system would not run. Power stations would be shut down. Factories would come to a halt. Police would not cooperate in locating the invader's opponents.

Church leaders would preach about the duty to refuse to help the occupation forces (as happened in Holland under the Nazis). Teachers would refuse to introduce enemy propaganda into the schools (as happened in Norway under the Nazis).

Disciplined, trained, nonviolent resisters would face the invader's clubs and bayonets with courage. If assaulted, others would take their place as soon as they were struck down (as happened in India under the British). If the invaders decided to teach a lesson through terror and began to fire on the unarmed resisters, many would be killed or wounded. Some would be terror-stricken for a while. But as the news of the massacre spread, public indignation against the troops would be powerful (as happened in Iran under the Shah). Many of the soldiers themselves would see this action as the opposite of the heroic battles they were prepared to fight for patriotic motives.

The courage of the civilians would surprise the invaders. Individual soldiers would begin talking about it among themselves. They were not trained to handle this kind of opposition. All the while people would be telling them they are not welcome and should go home. This might begin to appear reasonable to the invading forces. Their morale, perhaps after an initial display of military power, would begin to deteriorate. Some would have to be withdrawn and replaced with fresh troops (as happened in Czechoslovakia under the Soviets).

In addition to the nonviolent resistance inside the country, efforts would be made to influence public opinion in the invader's homeland. This could be done through sympathizers, through international agencies, and through the media, if the media is not completely government controlled. The resulting dissention at home would put additional pressure on the government to withdraw its forces (as happened in the United States during the Vietnam war).

The international community would be asked to intervene. Diplomatic pressures and economic sanctions would be imposed on the invading country (as happened to the Soviet Union during the Afghanistan occupation).

The nonviolent campaign would probably stretch on for a period of years. It would meet aggression with social, economic, political, and cultural weapons, not with military force. Those who practice it would never become passive in the face of the unjust occupation. Their courage, determination, and skill in the techniques of nonviolent action would intensify and spread until the invader finally understood that there was no fruit to this victory and decide to withdraw.

Precedents

The governments of Holland, Norway, and Sweden have commissioned studies on how nonviolent defense could be employed by developed nations in the 1980's. A long history of experiences in successful nonviolent resistance forms the basis for the conviction that this kind of defense can be effective.

Local opposition to Spanish rule in the Low Countries in the latter part of the 16th century involved years of public protests. These succeeded in weakening Spanish control so much that the king felt compelled to restore it by force. This proved impossible.

Civilian resistance was widely practiced by the American colonists in their move for independence. For more than a decade their actions were nonviolent. George Washington led a campaign to close down the courts in opposition to the Stamp Act, a classic example of the technique of noncooperation. Thomas Jefferson persuaded the Virginia House of Burgesses to declare a day of fasting and prayer for independence, another nonviolent tactic used much later by Gandhi.

By 1775 the rule of the British was practically nonexistent in 9 of the 13 colonies. Nonviolent tactics had gained effective independence. But a fringe group of hotheads had been talking violence all along. When shooting broke out in Lexington and Concord, the Revolutionary War began. It dragged on for 8 years.

Gene Sharp argues that the Revolutionary War actually prolonged the struggle for independence. That it succeeded at all was due in large measure to the progress the nonviolent movement had made over the previous decade.[7]

A century later and a continent away, the Hungarian people mounted a nonviolent campaign against the Austrian emperor who was trying to subdue them. They organized a boycott of Austrian goods, refused to pay Austrian taxes, and would not accept Austrian soldiers on their soil. These tactics led the emperor to grant Hungary a separate constitution and semi-autonomy.

Although the Finns used military measures (which were unsuccessful) to defend against the Soviet army in 1939, Finnish resistance to Russian rule 40 years earlier had been largely nonviolent. Finnish officials from 1898 to 1905 refused to sign legal papers. Judges would not take account of Russian law. Petitions were circulated, public protests organized. Teachers advocated that their students practice passive resistance. The Lutheran clergy preached it from their pulpits. The results were a 2-year period of independence, and the groundwork for establishing the Finnish republic a decade later.

The Central American nation of Costa Rica took the first step toward civilian defense when it disbanded its army in 1949. Since then it has succeeded in settling disputes with its neighbors by the international machinery of diplomacy and the Organization of American States.

The former British colony of the Gold Coast gained independence in 1957 as the nation of Ghana after a 10-year, largely nonviolent, struggle led by Kwane Nkrumah. So in 1964 did Zambia, galvanized by Kenneth Kaunda. Both men consistently adapted Gandhi's tactics to their African milieu.

Conclusion

A skeptical reporter once asked Gandhi how he would use nonviolence against the atom bomb. Gandhi replied:

> I will not go into shelter. I will come out in the open and let the pilot see I have not a trace of ill will against him. The pilot will not see our faces from his great height, I know. But the longing in our hearts—that he will come to no harm—would reach up to him and his eyes would be opened.[8]

If Gandhi's answer seems less than satisfactory, the question itself was impossible. When the button is pushed, it is too late for nonviolence, or any other defense. Nonviolent action must be initiated before the bombs are launched.

Although it is not yet widely known and still less widely practiced, active nonviolent work for peace and justice has great potential as a realistic alternative to war in the nuclear age.

Martin Luther King, prophetically, saw this back in 1964. "More and more people,'" he wrote, "have begun to conceive of this powerful ethic as a necessary way of life in a world where the wildly accelerated development of nuclear power has brought into being weapons that can annihilate all humanity." Nonviolence, which he saw as the answer to the needs of Black Americans, he also saw as "the answer to the most desperate need of all humanity."[9]

At first hearing, there is a tendency to be put off by the presumed inefficacy of nonviolence. The haunting question, "Will it work?" causes a momentary pause. There is sufficient evidence that nonviolence works about as often as, and considerably better than, violence, measured both in terms of casualties suffered and results achieved. But whether or not it works all the time, nonviolence is still the way demanded by truth.

Gandhi once said that nonviolence should be practiced not because it works, but because it is right.

It has worked in a profound way for centuries. It has changed minds and hearts, converted oppressors, saved lives, liberated nations. But ultimately nonviolence is to be judged not by the criteria of pragmatism, but by its agreement with a higher Law. As the Catholic monk Thomas Merton wrote, "Nonviolence is not for power but for truth. . . . Nonviolence is not primarily the language of efficacy, but the language of *kairos*"[10] — a special time for reaching and inspiring the human soul.

5   DEMYTHOLOGIZING THE ENEMY

The age of nations is past. The task before us now, if we would not perish, is to shake off our ancient prejudices, and to build the earth.

— Teilhard de Chardin

To meet the challenges of the nuclear age, a new vision of the human family is necessary. The nuclear threat hanging over the world reveals the inadequacy of the old vision of people grouped together in nation-states, prepared to defend their way of life by violence.

In the old vision nations are sovereign, independent, autonomous political entities. They coexist, usually, in a tentative truce, broken sometimes when one of them acts like a hostile aggressor. In the old vision, the world has some characteristics of a community, but its predominant features are of a jungle.

A nation may for a time join with others in a political or military alliance. Representatives of many nations may come together to try to prevent war by dealing with common problems. The United Nations, although one of the most helpful institutions in history for preventing war, is based on the old vision of sovereign states. The U.N. has only as much authority as its members give it, and they give it very little.

In the old vision a nation must ultimately rely on violence, or the threat of it, for its security.

The old vision of national defense stops functioning at the nuclear stage, because use of these weapons is equivalent to national suicide. They are procured in the name of defense, but if used their result is not defense but mutual destruction.

The old vision is not only obsolete, it is self-contradictory at the nuclear stage. It must yield either to an acknowledged death wish, or to a new vision.

An Ancient Prejudice

But the old vision is persistent. It has the characteristics of what the French Jesuit paleontologist, Pierre Teilhard de Chardin, called an ancient prejudice. In 1937 Teilhard wrote about "the passionate concern for our common destiny which draws the thinking part of life ever further onward."[1]

This universal concern for all people, he saw, has strong roots. "In principle there is no feeling which has a firmer foundation in nature or greater power." But he was also painfully aware, a half century ago, of the obstacles that hindered universal concern. "In fact there is also no feeling which awakens so belatedly, since it can become explicit only when our consciousness has expanded beyond the broadening, but still far too restricted circles of family, country and race."

The chief obstacle to developing a transnational, transracial vision is the human propensity to take most seriously the realities close at hand. One's attention tends to be absorbed by the people, places, and problems encountered directly in day-to-day living.

Another factor is the extension of self-interest into family, friends, and nation. A person's own well-being is influenced by what happens to those nearby. The tendency to self-protection extends to protecting those others also.

Strangers are viewed with suspicion. They are different. They have strange customs. Perhaps they speak a different language. They may be of another race, or have unusual physical characteristics. Communication is difficult, if not impossible. Any interaction, stimulated by distrust, might well be competitive, if not violent, in the interest of self-protection from the perceived threat.

Original Sin

A particular religious strain in American culture provides reinforcement for these tendencies. In the United States there have been two mainstream interpretations of the biblical story of the original sin of Adam and Eve.

One interpretation sees original sin as an essential corruption of human nature, which is, as a consequence, fundamentally bad. People are accepted by God because of the redeeming death of Jesus Christ. They can be saved only when they turn to him.

This view, first articulated by Saint Augustine and given new impetus by Martin Luther and John Calvin during the Reformation, dominated religious thinking in the early years of the United States. It supported legends of the frontier hero who, properly humble before God, used his wits and strength to overcome the lawless, faithless villains who exploited decent, God-fearing people. It also supported the conviction that godless people anywhere in the world were corrupt, up to no good, and could legitimately be subdued by force if they became a threat.

A second interpretation understood original sin as a serious weakening of human nature, but not as its essential corruption. Human nature remains basically good, created by God. Christ's redemption restores its fundamental orientation toward God, with the final healing to take place after death.

This view, articulated by Saint Thomas Aquinas in the 13th century, became, after the Reformation, the basis of Roman Catholic understanding of human nature. It did not become part of the American theological mix until substantial numbers of Catholic immigrants entered the country at the end of the last century, too late to form part of the prevailing climate of opinion.

In this second understanding, human beings are weakened, but fundamentally decent. Violence is a result of the weakness, it is not an inevitable outcome of essential corruption. The most effective way of dealing with it is to bring out the inherent good in people, not increase the evil through counterviolence. Father Flanagan, founder of Boys Town, acting out of this model, said, "There's no such thing as a bad boy."

But the prevailing thought in the United States was Calvinistic, not Thomistic. Salvation, believed Calvin, came from God's will antecedent to any human decisions. Calvin's heirs, the Pilgrims and Puritans, Huguenots, Scots, Dutch, believed that earthly prosperity was a sign of God's favorable judgment. Poverty, on the other hand, was a sign of moral depravity, a testimony to the corruption caused by original sin.

Americans were prepared, then, toward the end of the nineteenth century, for the theory of social Darwinism: that in human society, as in the animal world, only the fittest survive. Those people and nations who prospered were a better breed, loved by God, and superior to the poor and the struggling.

If these others were not satisfied with their inferior state and tried to take from those who had prospered, they had to be stopped, by force if necessary.

President Lyndon Johnson expressed this view shortly after he took office. He told a group of reporters:

I grew up with Mexicans. They'll come right into your yard and take it over if you let them. And the next day they'll be on your porch, barefoot and weighing 130 pounds, and they'll take that, too. But if you say to 'em right at the start, "Hold on, just wait a minute," they'll know they're dealing with somebody who'll stand up. And after that you can get along fine.[2]

This was the same view he expressed when he visited the troops in Vietnam and told them to "nail the coonskin to the wall," because if these sorts of people were not put decisively in their place they will "sweep over the United States and take what we have." He was expressing the prevailing attitude of most Americans, who considered their nation outstanding, and the object of envy.

World Citizenship

But this cultural tendency to consider others as dangerous need not be decisive. It is possible to move beyond it, and deliberately cultivate a new vision. The world's philosophical and religious geniuses had this new vision. They understood the oneness of humankind.

Siddhartha Gautama, the Buddha, 500 years before Christ, felt universal compassion. "May all breathing things, all who are born, all individuals of whatever kind be free from enmity, affliction and anxiety, may they live happily."[3] His hope flowed from a realization of the common vitality shared beyond the boundaries of family, caste or kingdom.

"I am not an Athenian or a Greek," said Socrates on his deathbed, "but a citizen of the world."

Jesus taught that the supreme guide to life was love of neighbor, who was anyone in need, regardless of religious or national differences. Just before he died he prayed for all believers, "that all of them may be one, Father, just as you are in me and I am in you" (Jn 17:21). His follower, Paul, wrote that "there is neither Jew nor Greek, slave nor free, male nor female, for you are all one in Christ Jesus" (Gal. 3:26). Paul saw the essential unity of everyone "in Christ Jesus," a unity that transcended racial, class, and sex differences.

Six centuries later the prophet Mohammed expressed a similar view in the Koran. "The believers are surely brothers. Reconcile them one to another as your brothers and fear God, that you may receive his grace" (49:10).

The transnational and transracial unity inspired by these words changed the life of a 20th century follower of Mohammed, the American black leader Malcolm X. After his return from Mecca in 1964, he said that what had impressed him most about his pilgrimage was "the brotherhood! The people of all races, colors, from all over the world coming together as one!"[4] After this transforming experience, Malcolm felt deeply that the secret to racial accord lay in reconciliation, not retaliation.

Nationalism

The most rigid block to the new vision is the 20th century nation-state, which functions as the largest closed circle in the lives of its members. The modern nation draws people's loyalties out from their immediate spheres of family and those interest groups that are the contemporary counterparts of tribes.

An isolated individual looks on life as a challenge to be faced alone, in an environment, human as well as physical, that may well be threatening. One's sense of personal inadequacy is soothed by pride in the achievement of one's nation. The security of the home from predators within the society, and the security of the nation from predators outside, become of paramount importance. The nation then provides the outer limit to one's personal loyalties. The result is a nationalism based on pride and possessions, accompanied by suspicion toward other nations.

President Truman told a visitor at the end of World War II that the Russians "would soon be put into their place, and the United States would then take the lead in running the world in a way that the world ought to be run."[5] The assumption that the United States knows better than any other nation how "the world ought to be run" is indicative of this kind of nationalism.

When love of country encourages killing for the furthering of its vital interests, it becomes dangerous.

A monument in Brussels honoring those who died defending Belgium in two world wars bears the inscription, "Salus Patriae Suprema Lex." The safety of the fatherland is the supreme law. Not the will of God, not the welfare of the human family, not the ideals of truth and love, but the safety of the country is the supreme law.

The same thrust is implied in the motto of the armed forces of Spain, inscribed on the entrance to military bases, *Todos por la patria:* Everything for the Fatherland. Being willing to give everything, and do anything, for the fatherland implies respect for no higher law. The nation is at the very top of one's value system and one is prepared to go to any lengths to defend it.

The Florentine Renaissance political philosopher Niccolo Machiavelli expressed this implication forcefully. "When it is a question of the safety of the country, no account should be taken of what is just or unjust, merciful or cruel, laudable or shameful, but without regard to anything else, that course is to be unswervingly pursued which will save the life and maintain the liberty of the fatherland."[6]

These dynamics dominated the world through the first half of the 20th century. Even before the shock of World War II, Teilhard saw that they must, and would, be replaced. "Life can progress on our planet in the future (and nothing will prevent it from progressing, not even its own internal servitudes) by throwing down the barriers which still wall off human activity."

Two important forces undermined the rigidity of the psychological barriers of national boundaries. The electronics revolution, with the world-wide expansion of telecommunication networks, brought the sounds and sights of far away peoples into hundreds of millions of homes. The transportation explosion, particularly the passenger jet aircraft, brought rapid intercontinental movement within the economic means of millions. The seeds of international awareness and transcultural appreciation were sown widely.

A particularly disillusioning encounter with one's nation, such as a war of exploitation or repressive internal violence, could act as a catalyst to bring a person to a flash of post-national consciousness.

The New Vision

When the barrier of nationalism comes down, one wanders at first in a strange and beautiful landscape, where once familiar landmarks take on a different hue, and once strange and forbidding areas become suddenly familiar. One then looks for a new orientation. The old one will never again be adequate.

The first element of the new fix is the broad concern for the whole human family. One has a new appreciation of the "joys, hopes, griefs and anxieties," the major concerns identified by the Second Vatican Council, of people different in language, customs and appearance. These become signs of shared humanity. The energies, tragedies and triumphs of people become much more important than their national identity.

So does the shared dependence on the earth's natural resources, as Gerald and Patricia Mische of Global Education Associates pointed out. "We are unalterably bound together. We share a common dependency on one earth system. We stand together in relationship with one air, water, land and life-support system. We have the same needs, the same potentialities, the same capacities for participating in destruction or for participating in creation."[7]

Then comes a heightened appreciation of family, friends, and community. The desire for warmth and sharing with persons close at hand is no longer a blind groping for intimacy to counteract the anxiety felt by an autonomous individual. It is recognition of the essential incompleteness of all human beings. The need to interact with those close at hand complements the reaching out to those beyond the circles.

"As we enter the global phase of social evolution, it becomes obvious that each one of us has two countries—his own and the planet earth," wrote biologist Rene Dubos. "We cannot feel at home on earth if we do not continue to love and cultivate our own garden. And conversely, we can hardly feel comfortable in our garden if we do not care for the planet earth as our collective home."[8]

The dominant trend that put overwhelming weight on the immediate, on the interests of the nation, must be counterbalanced by concern for neighbors far away. On one level, these neighbors may be citizens of another nation, but on another and more important level, they are co-citizens in the global village.

The new vision calls for a relativization of national sovereignty. No longer can it be absolute. No longer can a nation legitimately claim that its internal affairs are no one else's business. Aleksandr Solzhenitsyn has said,

There are no internal affairs left on our crowded earth! And mankind's sole salvation lies in everyone making everything his business: in the people of the East being vitally concerned with what is thought in the West, the people of the West vitally concerned with what goes on in the East.[9]

The human condition of solidarity demands the interaction of peoples, regardless of national boundaries. It is the only way in which the true human community can be built. It is the only way to true peace, as the World Conference on Religion and Peace, meeting in Princeton in 1979, declared.

World community, built on love, freedom, justice and truth, is another name for peace. It is the goal of all our strivings. It is not a utopian dream. . . . We believe that peace in the world community is not only possible, but is the way of life for human beings on earth.[10]

True Patriotism

The feeling of pride and love of one's country is a common phenomenon. Patriotism is encouraged all over the world. The national anthem sung on special occasions, reverence for a country's flag, stories highlighting noble events of its past, these are part of everyone's cultural surroundings. They are part of what sociologists Peter Berger and Thomas Luckmann call the process of legitimation, explaining and justifying what goes on in a society.

True patriotism values a country for its ideals and its potential for decency. Love of one's country, respect for its valuable traditions, and a feeling of closeness to fellow citizens, are important correctives to the common tendency toward selfishness.

Patriotism is a noble sentiment. It becomes unhealthy only when it is accompanied by a dislike of other countries and their people. Vatican Council II encouraged people of good will all over the world to put patriotism in its proper perspective.

Citizens should develop a generous and loyal devotion to their country, but without any narrowing of mind. In other words, they must always look simultaneously to the welfare of the whole human family, which is tied together by the manifold bonds linking races, peoples and nations.[11]

The Enemy

Because a world citizen with the new vision is simultaneously a citizen of a particular country, a realistic appraisal of that country's enemies is necessary.

Enemy is a powerful concept. It evokes fear and hostility, and, if the conditions are right, leads to war. When the label of enemy is placed on another country, the relationship with that country takes on an added strain.

The United States' leadership portrays its major enemy as the Soviet Union. Public opinion, swayed by the enemy image, supports the spending of additional billions of dollars and the production of sophisticated superweapons.

Students of religious language are familiar with the category of myth for an image that captures something of reality and has power to move people deeply. Myth in this sense is not the same as legend or fairy tale. It is a pictorial way of presenting something that cannot be expressed so readily or forcefully in any other way. It may or may not be based on facts. It may or may not be completely true. But it is important because it can affect people significantly, move them emotionally. The Soviet Union as enemy is a myth in this sense of the word.

The German scripture scholar Rudolf Bultmann developed a technique for interpreting some of the images (or myths in this sense) of the bible by giving their meaning for human life in concrete, existential language. The process, which he called demythologizing, did not do away with the myth, but rather explained the reality behind it. That process can profitably be applied to the Soviet Union as enemy.

Social psychologist Morton Deutsch has identified three elements that must be present for what is technically called intergroup hostility: enmity between societies or nations. They are contact, visibility, and competition.[12]

In order for the Soviet Union to be perceived as hostile to the United States, the two nations must first have contact with each other. This they have had abundantly in the last 50 years. During World War II the two nations were uneasy allies. After the war their encounters have been worldwide, as each has attempted to extend its influence as widely as possible.

The second element, visibility, means that the other nation has to be seen as significantly different. From the American perspective, Russia's economic system and social organization are state controlled, not free. Its official ideology is Marxism, a worldview that is atheistic, materialistic, and communistic. This contrasts dramatically with the stated American worldview, which is religious, humanitarian, and capitalistic. The Soviet Union is seen as desiring world domination. The United States presents itself as desiring freedom for all. The Soviet Union is presented as ruthless, the United States as benign.

The third element, competition, locks in the hostility. The United States and the Soviet Union, the two most powerful nations in the history of the human race, compete for power and prestige everywhere in the world. Occasionally, U.S. presidents officially acknowledge the competition. President Carter did so in a speech at Georgia Tech in early 1979. He said:

> Our relationship with the Soviet Union is a mixture of cooperation and competition. I have no more difficult and delicate task than to balance these two. I cannot and I will not let the pressures of inevitable competition overwhelm possibilities for cooperation any more than I will let cooperation blind us to the realities of competition.[13]

Sometimes the competition becomes heated. Since 1945 United States military forces, or their surrogates, have engaged Soviet-influenced forces in eastern Europe, Korea, Cuba, Vietnam, and parts of Africa and Latin America. Clandestine operatives of both nations have been involved in covert hostilities around the world.

The enemy image causes Americans to evaluate Soviet actions negatively. Its domination of Eastern Europe is called imperialistic, its invasion of Afghanistan, expansionistic. There is little effort to probe for the real causes of these events.

Demythologizing

But no one is a prisoner of this frame of reference. It is possible to understand Soviet international behavior against a different background and give it a different interpretation. The process of demythologizing begins with this effort.

The Soviet Union is a nation with a large and diverse population. It is struggling with an economic system that works better than the one of the Czars, but not as well as the capitalism of the West. Its leaders have to maintain the economy, and keep their people under control. When internal stability is threatened, they tend to take strong corrective action.

This, according to the Soviet news media, explains their invasion of Afghanistan. Unrest in that border country promised to spill over into the neighboring Soviet republic of Tashkent, many of whose people have ethnic and religious ties with the Afghanis. The purpose of the invasion was to preserve order on the border in the interests of peace at home.

Other dynamics are involved in the domination of Eastern Europe. The Soviet Union lost 20 million people in World War II. One out of every nine persons in the country was killed as a result of the brutal Nazi invasion. After the war, the Soviets attempted to secure a protective zone of countries in Eastern Europe to prevent such an invasion and such devastation from happening again.

From their geopolitical perspective they are surrounded by hostile powers. On their eastern border is China, a nation of 1 billion people, which, Russians feel, is in need of new territories for its growing population. China has been sending out hostile signals toward the Soviet Union since the early 1960's.

To the west lie Germany, which invaded in 1941, France, which invaded in 1812, and the rest of Europe, which supplied troops to put down the 1917 revolution and today has modern weapons aimed at the Soviet Union.

The United States would be in a similar plight if both Canada and Mexico were large, powerful, well-armed, and hostile neighbors.

Besides the threatening powers on both sides of its land mass, the Soviet Union faces a threat from halfway around the world. The United States has strategic nuclear missiles that can destroy every city in the Soviet Union several dozen times. The threat from the United States is particularly severe. From the dawn of the nuclear age until the mid-1970's, American nuclear superiority was overwhelming. "The present generation of Soviet political and military leaders," noted Robert Kaiser, former Moscow correspondent for the Washington Post, "grew up looking into the uncomfortable end of the nuclear barrel."[14]

After the Cuban missile crisis in 1962, Soviet leaders vowed that future confrontations with the United States would never be resolved in the same humiliating way. They embarked on a military buildup that enabled them to reach a rough equality in nuclear weapons, and also to project their power into other parts of the world.

They were successful in the nuclear race, reaching the stage of parity where they can destroy the United States as thoroughly as the United States can destroy them. Both sides acknowledged this fundamental equality in negotiating two strategic arms limitation treaties.

But the Soviet Union has not been as successful as the United States in extending its influence around the world. A 1977 study by the Brookings Institution reported that in the 30 years between 1945 and 1975, the United States had deployed its military forces abroad for political impact on at least 215 different occasions, not including Korea and Vietnam. These were shows of force by ships, aircraft, or troops that involved force or the threat of force. Typical incidents included the positioning of a naval task force off Brazil in early 1964 to support a coup by that country's armed forces against the left-leaning government of President Joao Goulart.

During the same 30-year period, the Soviet Union deployed its military units on similar missions on 115 occasions.

Although Soviet efforts have met with some successes, as in Vietnam and earlier in Cuba, their failures also have been outstanding. Soviet forces were expelled from Egypt, Sudan, and Somalia. Richard Barnet has pointed out that "just as in military hardware the Soviet Union has been three to five years behind the United States in developing major new weapons systems, so in acquiring the political accoutrements of superpower status—'show the flag' naval power, proxy armies, military aid—the Soviets have been imitators."[15]

The process of demythologizing does not do away with the concept of enmity, nor does it lead to the view that all enemies are really misperceived friends. Rather, it sees the policies of other nations in their own historical and political contexts, just as it sees the policies of one's own nation in its own contexts. Each country threatens the very existence of the other. The only two genuine superpowers in the world, nations built with a prodigious output of creative energy, face each other poised for mutually assured destruction. The enmity is indeed present, but it is not one-sided.

Within the parameters of the nuclear confrontation, Soviet and American leaders are trying to increase their nations' power and prestige.

In any event the citizens, the people, of the Soviet Union are not genuine enemies. Their leaders may or may not be, depending on how far they are willing to go to achieve their international designs. But U.S. leaders are also engaged in the international power game. A realistic perspective on enemies must focus on the genuine causes of international tensions, and not simply on the label enemy when it is applied to a whole country.

Truth Before Loyalty

Demythologizing the Soviets as enemy helps one perceive the real enemy today, the threat of wholesale nuclear slaughter. The French philosopher Albert Camus once wrote, "All I ask is that, in the midst of a murderous world, we agree to reflect on murder and to make a choice. After that, we can distinguish those who accept the consequences of being murderers themselves or the accomplices of murderers, and those who refuse to do so with all their force and being."[16]

Camus' insight shines out as a beacon in the complex and morally murky world of the late 20th century. Pilate's age-old question, what is truth, is particularly difficult to answer in the complicated and confused arena of international manuevering. But if, with Camus, we can identify murder and preparations for murder — and nuclear weapons fit the category preeminently — then we can choose on which side of those preparations to stand.

The choice to become, or resist becoming, accomplices to the mass murder represented by nuclear weapons provides a rare moment of truth. If the decision to resist takes one beyond national loyalties, so much the worse for national loyalties. The truth, at least this once, seems clear.

Loyalty to community, company, or country should never obscure the imperatives of facing these facts. Loyalty can cover a multitude of sins. Truth demands that loyalty be put in second place when the good of people is at stake. And so the choice is truth and life, before loyalty and death. Then the real work for peace begins.

Conclusion

The vision of reality to guide one through the nuclear age includes all of the human race, in splendid diversity, forming a single human family, beyond the boundaries of race, creed, and nation. Conflicts will exist, as they do in all families, but they will not be artificially instigated by the propagation of enemy images based on national citizenship. Loyalty to family, friends, and nation will be lived with proper adjustments made for a broader loyalty to the entire human family. Inspired by this vision, one can make the necessary adjustments in personal life and play an active, creative part in bringing the vision to reality.

6　PERSONAL NONVIOLENCE

The choice today is no longer between violence and nonviolence. It is either nonviolence or nonexistence.

—Martin Luther King, Jr.

The existential question is, finally, What can I do? Everything. Everything, but not in the sense that a single individual can do whatever is necessary to turn back the nuclear tide. But everything a person does, every act of the day, can be done in a nonviolent, or less violent, way.

It is possible to approach the conflicts that lace one's life with the positive mental attitude of trying to resolve them without resort to violence. In this way, with the struggle to overcome fear, to master the surges of anger, to react constructively to hostility, one's life becomes part of the pattern of peacemaking that can spread throughout the world. Every individual act of nonviolence helps to create and spread that pattern.

A journey of a thousand miles begins with one step, observed Confucius. If many people are to be convinced of the validity and effectiveness of nonviolent defense, a few have to be convinced first. Then it can spread.

It is important to think big, to think globally, even though most of one's life is lived small, locally. On both levels, globally and locally, the words of A.J. Muste, founder of the Fellowship of Reconciliation, are axiomatic: "There is no way to peace; peace is the way."

Quietly, privately, without making waves, anyone convinced that the dominant political forces in the nuclear age are idolatrous, that the moral atmosphere is poisonous, can begin to reorient personal attitudes.

Spirituality

The foundation for effective peacemaking is a healthy spirituality. This means one's inner life, life of the mind and heart, is nourished by ideals of wholesome, healing human possibilities that are congruent with the basic flow of reality. It means also that one drinks deeply of sources that inspire and communicate strength.

For some, an adequate spiritual life will grow around prayer and Scripture reading. Others will find their nourishment in worship, or meditative exchanges with committed persons. Many will be inspired by the wisdom of the great prophets of nonviolence: Gandhi, Martin Luther King, Tolstoy, Daniel Berrigan, Dorothy Day.

A sound spirituality for peacemaking develops empathy for the poor, the oppressed, those that suffer from violence anywhere in the world, including one's family and friends. It also involves a continual reflection on one's lifestyle, and a constant adjustment of the desire for comfort and security with the call to detachment and witness.

One's spirituality is never complete. Efforts to sustain and develop it must continue. The alternative is to give up the struggle and sink into moral apathy.

The dominant theme will be hope. People can change, structures can be improved, conflicts can be resolved, swords can be beaten into plowshares. Nuclear destruction is not inevitable. Neither is personal violence. No one is a prisoner of the past. This universe, this world, and the people who inhabit it, are fundamentally good. A sober, realistic hope is the driving force of a peacemaker's life.

Study

Only slightly less important than spiritual development is the attempt to achieve a degree of competence in some of the critical areas of the nuclear age, including techniques of nonviolent conflict resolution. In order to engage more effectively, a person should have some technical knowledge. Knowledge could be about any number of aspects: power and deployment of nuclear weapons, the international arms race, military strengths and strategies. Awareness of the basic dynamics of national and international economics is helpful, so is some knowledge of the strengths and weaknesses of the principal political systems in the world.

A peacemaker should know about nonviolent alternatives to the forces of oppression. The real work for peace in the nuclear age must take the direction of applying these alternatives, of making them work in the concrete circumstances of personal and political life. Techniques of nonviolent action, principles on which these techniques rest, and historical precedents, need to be understood. This is essential knowledge for peace. It calls for study, for time spent seriously investigating the realities that confront us and the ways of dealing with them.

A peacemaker need not be as knowledgeable as government experts or university scholars. But the knowledge should be sufficiently extensive and accurate to ensure that he or she will be taken seriously, not dismissed as blowing in the wind or floating on naive idealism.

The shifting day-to-day world scene should also be kept in sight. Changing conditions continuously affect the forces critical for violence or peace. The Swiss theologian Karl Barth once said that the proper way to do theology in these times is with the bible in one hand and the daily newspaper in the other.

Most of the men and women at the controls of the political, economic, and military machinery of the nuclear age are well aware of what is going on in the world, and are adjusting their operations accordingly. Peacemakers, who seek alternative ways of dealing with conflicts, or the opportunity to build new and more effective structures, must have sufficient insight into these events.

Self-Awareness

Concurrently with study will come an increased understanding of what kind of creatures humans are. The assumption that people are selfish and greedy, and will prey on their neighbors given the opportunity, will come under increasing doubt. The belief that human nature is innately aggressive is open for serious debate.[1]

Some important thinkers have supported it. The philosopher Thomas Hobbes described human life as "solitary, poor, hasty, brutish, and short." Sigmund Freud thought that human beings possess a drive for destruction and hatred, derived from what he called a death instinct.

The ethologist Konrad Lorenz theorized that this instinct was operative in the earliest humans. He pointed out that alongside of the first traces of fire lie mutilated human bones, from which he concluded "Peking Man, who learned to preserve fire, used it to roast his brothers."

In a popular 1966 book, *The Territorial Imperative,* naturalist Robert Ardrey saw evidence that the immediate ancestors of the human race made tools, and used some of them to bash in the skulls of baboons. Therefore, he concluded, human beings are killers by nature. "Man is a predator whose natural instinct is to kill with a weapon." This instinct is reinforced, he wrote, by "an innate compulsion to gain and defend exclusive territory or property."

Zoologist Desmond Morris thought that "man's intelligence will never be able to rule his raw animal nature nor control his biological urge to aggression."

Political scientist Gunter Lewy explained that the ubiquity of war shows that violence is an inescapable human phenomenon. The proper approach, he says, is not to try to eliminate war, but to control its excesses.

That human nature is innately aggressive, and that this is an important cause of war, has long been disputed. The assertion about ubiquity proves nothing. Slavery was fairly widespread until a century or two ago. Its defenders said it was a natural part of the human condition. Child abuse is perhaps as ubiquitous as war, but it too is seen as a social evil and efforts are underway to eliminate it.

Psychologist Rollo May analyzed violence not as the result of an innate instinct, but a reaction to frustration, an expression of impotence.

Anthropologist Ashley Montague asserted that, while it is true that human beings have genetic limitations, they have no innate instincts for violence. Behavior is learned. Survival places a higher premium on cooperation than on aggression, and so the history of the human race is characterized by constant efforts to get along with one another. Violence is exceptional, according to Montague.

Margaret Mead, on the basis of her anthropological studies of a number of traditional societies, came to the conclusion that "War is only an invention, not a biological necessity." She found that the Eskimos did not even have a concept of war. Not just the word, but the idea of organized violence was lacking in their culture. The same was true of the Lepchas of Sikhim. Some peoples who know about war, like Hopi Pueblo Indians, label it as undesirable, and communicate a negative attitude toward it among their people.

Economist Kenneth Boulding has written, "Insofar as aggression or territoriality play a part in human culture—and they do —each generation learns them from the previous generation and perhaps in a lesser degree from its own physical environment and random events."

Biologist Rene Dubos has pointed out that not only violence, but also revulsion to violence is "one of the hallmarks of human history. . . . While it is obvious that many men are killers, it is equally true that many more are not." He concludes that "the potentiality for aggressiveness is indeed part of man's genetic constitution just as it is part of the genetic constitution of all animal species. But the manifestation of all genetic potentialities is shaped by past experiences and present circumstances."

On balance, there is some evidence to suggest that human beings have an innate instinct for violence. There is other evidence, at least equally compelling, showing that violence is learned, not instinctive.

When one is faced with persuasive theories on both sides of a question, the direction in which one leans is guided more by personal predilection than by the power of objective truth.

Everyone feels some degree of personal insecurity or inadequacy in the face of the day's challenges. One way of coping with a world lacking warmth, love, and understanding is to try to impose as much control on that world as possible. The person can overcome feelings of frustration and intimidation by seeking power, trying to dominate others, manipulating them for his or her own satisfaction.

Recognition of this drive in oneself makes one alert to signs of it in others. It leads to the assumption that hostile acts are to be expected, and can be checked only by an exercise of superior power.

Personal insecurity can work itself out in another direction. Experience may have taught that getting along with others creates the best atmosphere for coping with life. Getting along involves giving up some of one's desires. It involves openness to the energy of others. Approached in this way, others will almost invariably prove to be friendly and helpful. Cooperation, not competition, is seen to be the key for making the most of personal resources. This attitude predisposes a person to choose the second answer, that violence is not innate but learned.

Communication

Study and self-awareness are helped greatly by sharing ideas with other people. Discussions, exchanging viewpoints, and learning what others consider important helps focus and clarify what one is dealing with privately. These experiences reinforce one's resolve, and encourage further work.

Communication should also take place with those who are not of like mind in peace questions. The exchange need not be abrasive or polemical. One hopes it will not be abusive or defensive.

Its purpose is to share what has been discovered, and also to learn the approaches of those who support the present systems of violence. A better understanding of their ways of thinking is important if the problems of the nuclear age are to be dealt with adequately.

This kind of communication can also be a way of influencing and even creating public opinion. Talking with others strengthens their impression that alternative ideas are abroad and are taken seriously by serious people. Letters to the editor of local newspapers, letters to national officials, all have power to make known the existence of a peace constituency.

President John Kennedy once told a visiting group of Quakers that if they could mobilize the American people to shout themselves hoarse for disarmament, he would be pleased to lead the crusade. Because government officials depend to a significant degree on public opinion, creation of a climate favorable to such peace moves as disarmament is an important reason for persevering in communication.

Nonviolence of Individuals

Since active, positive nonviolence is the most promising alternative to war in the nuclear age, any individual can begin to work toward this alternative by consciously allowing nonviolence to permeate all the phases of life. Through conscious effort and practice it can become almost a reflex response. This can happen when a person attempts to apply the principles of nonviolence in relationships with family and friends, in business exchanges, in one's career and professional life, and in chance encounters that have unpleasant possibilities.

All these areas can be riddled with psychological and structural violence. Aggressive behavior, competition, and winning through intimidation can and often do characterize personal dealings, unless one consciously pursues a nonviolent course.

The chances of resolving a conflict nonviolently are better if it is viewed as a problem to be solved jointly, rather than as a contest to be won or lost.

Gandhi compared the nonviolent campaigner to a soldier who needs discipline and training to act properly under provocation. Nonviolent discipline can be self-imposed. Much of the training can come from trying to act nonviolently in everyday life.

The following tips on how to act nonviolently were adapted from *Peace by Peace,* the newspaper of Northern Ireland's Peace People.

1. *Don't be frightened.* Fear is perceived, and encourages a hostile party to continue the undesired activity. It is difficult not to be afraid in a confrontation, but not impossible. It is important to breathe deeply, to keep talking slowly, and to maintain eye contact.

2. *Don't be frightening.* Someone about to commit an act of violence is likely to be more fearful than the person being attacked. Abrupt gestures can feed that fear. So can saying anything threatening, critical, or hostile. A calm response to reassure an attacker can lessen the tension and give time for a peaceful resolution.

3. *Don't behave like a victim.* Someone in the process of committing an act of violence has strong expectations how the victim will behave. Acting differently, in a non-threaten-

ing manner, can interrupt the flow of events and avoid the violence. A woman who woke up in the middle of the night to find a strange man by her bed had the presence of mind to say right away, "What time is it?" The threatening stranger, momentarily off guard, answered her question. The conversation that followed defused a potentially harmful encounter.

4. *Seek to befriend the other person's better nature.* This is at the heart of nonviolent action. Even the most brutal and brutalized have some spark of decency that the nonviolent person can reach. The task is to help a person see that an intended act of hostility is inconsistent with the kind of person the opponent wishes to be.

5. *Be firm in the face of violence.* The most frequent mistake persons who wish to be nonviolent make is that they do not resist firmly enough. Passivity usually further angers a violent person. But sometimes an aggressive person is so upset that even a mild form of resistance can be explosive. The situation has to be played by ear. The best guideline is to resist as firmly as possible without escalating the anger or the violence.

6. *Keep talking. Keep listening.* The hostile person should be encouraged to talk. It's best not to argue with him/her, but at the same time the impression should not be conveyed that there is agreement with assertions that are cruel or immoral. The listening is more important than what is said. The talking should be kept going, and be kept calm.

The heart of nonviolent action, in everyday life as well as in organized campaigns, is respect for the humanity of those who are temporarily opponents. The key is to avoid an angry or harmful response, and to communicate affirmation and support rather than fear or a threat.

Probably this is what happened when Jesus once faced a hostile crowd that wanted to kill him. It was early in his ministry.

Jesus had spoken in the synagogue in Nazareth, identifying himself with the signs of the coming kingdom of God. Luke says that the people of Nazareth were very upset by this synagogue sermon. "When they heard this, all in the synagogue were filled with wrath. And they rose up and put him out of the city, and led him to the brow of the hill on which their city was built, that they might throw him headlong" (Luke 4:28-29).

But the crowd did not push Jesus over that cliff. Luke does not explain what happened, only that "passing through the midst of them he went away" (Luke 4:30).

That is a mysterious verse. Perhaps Jesus escaped in some supernatural, mystical way. Perhaps angels came and quieted the crowd. Perhaps Jesus used a superhuman power of hypnosis to mesmerize the crowd while he walked through it to safety.

But it is more likely that what happened was a result not of a supernatural intervention but of self-control, the strength of his personal presence. When people were about to do violence to him, instead of reacting in fear, instead of reacting with counterviolence, Jesus reacted in a calm, quiet, self-possessed way and somehow the people who were about to kill him stopped acting violently toward him.

A story is told in Israel about a man named Joseph Abileah, the founder of the Haifa Symphony Orchestra. He had a similar experience with a hostile crowd. Some years ago he was in an Arab village talking with people. Other villagers crowded around him, and said, "We are going to kill you." Abileah asked them why. "We have orders to do so. You are Jewish and we are Arab, and our leaders have told us to kill every Jew that we see."

As a solitary man surrounded by a hostile crowd, Abileah knew that to resist would be futile. He also knew that to show signs of weakness would only encourage the crowd to overcome its timidity about doing this inhuman thing. So he asked how they were going to kill him. "We will throw you down a well." "Where is the well?" "Over there."

Abileah walked over to the well; the people followed, determined to kill him. By the time they reached the well, it was clear that the mood of the people was changing. They saw in him a human being who was not afraid, who was not hostile, who stood before them confident, courageous, willing to face death.

They hesitated. Instead of throwing him into the well, they asked themselves how to avoid this murder they felt obliged to inflict, but that they no longer wanted to commit.

Finally, a solution was discovered. They decided to make him a Moslem. Since he would no longer be Jewish, they would not have to kill him. They declared on the spot that Joseph Abileah was a Moslem, therefore no longer susceptible to death. He then passed through the midst of them and walked away.[2]

Positive Peace

Peace is more than the avoidance of killing, more than the cessation of war. Peace, as theologian Joseph Fahey has described it, involves not only a low level of physical and psychological violence, but also a high level of economic and social justice.[3] When the structures of a country prevent some people from obtaining enough food to avoid malnutrition, adequate housing to avoid exposure, and sufficient medical care to counteract disease, the system is inflicting violence on these people. That country is not peaceful. Though it may not be at war with other nations, it is at war with some of its people.

Peace is not just the absence of the quick killing through physical violence. It is also the absence of the slow killing through structural violence. It is a positive condition in which people are free, not exploited, living so they can grow to their full potential.

The vision of positive peace exerts a powerful pull. It focuses on meeting the needs of people wherever they are, regardless of the forces by which they are threatened. Any action along these lines is an act of peacemaking. "Peacemaking isn't something we ought to do in our spare time, it's something we need to do all the time. Action to alleviate world hunger (including that down the block) is peacemaking," as theologian Robert McAfee Brown has written. "Whatever enhances the well-being of the human family is peacemaking, the spreading of shalom."[4]

Individual nonviolent effort to bring about justice at any level is vitally important for peace. Effective peacemaking also calls for combined efforts. Forces pushing in the direction of war and structures perpetrating injustices are national and international in scope. To deal with them adequately, many skillful and dedicated people must cooperate, across national boundaries if necessary.

International Peace Groups

There are many international peace organizations that combine information with action, spirit with organization. Most, incidentally, have minimal or no membership fees. The advantages of belonging to one or another are numerous. Members have contact with like-minded people throughout the country and around the world. They receive news about activities for peace that they would not otherwise find in the newspaper. When actions for peace are undertaken, international resources are available to make the campaigns more effective.

A person may not be able to take part in many of the actions, but can contribute financial or moral support, and can receive an important feeling of solidarity with the movement.

The three groups described here have significant interest in a broad range of nonviolent actions for disarmament, social justice, human rights, and world order.

The Fellowship of Reconciliation is a religiously based, although nondenominational, pacifist organization. It describes itself as an association of men and women "who recognize the essential unity of all humanity and have joined together to explore the power of love and truth for resolving human conflict." It was founded in England in 1914 to provide support for conscientious objectors to military service. The United States branch was begun a year later. It now numbers over 100,000 members around the world, and has formally established branches in 25 countries.

The FOR's international center is in Alkmaar, Holland. Its American address is Box 271, Nyack, NY 10960.

The War Resisters League is a pacifist organization based on ethical and humanist, rather than religious, values. Anyone can join who signs its pledge: "War is a crime against humanity. We therefore are determined not to support any kind of war and to strive for the removal of all causes of war." It advocates Gandhian nonviolence as the method for creating a democratic society free from war, racism, and human exploitation. Founded in 1923, the WRL moved pacifism from its emphasis on individual resistance to an organized movement against the causes of war. It played a leadership role in the civil rights and peace movements of the 1960's and 1970's.

The WRL is the American affiliate of War Resisters International. Twenty-two other countries have branches, with the international headquarters located in London. Its address in the United States is 339 Lafayette St., New York, NY 10012.

Pax Christi, whose Latin name means "the peace of Christ," is a predominantly, although not exclusively, Roman Catholic movement for peace. It was founded at the end of World War II by a French bishop who wanted to promote reconciliation between French and German war veterans. While Pax Christi attracts many pacifists, this is not a condition for membership. Its aim is to be a broadly based coalition of persons who are committed to the belief that nonviolence must become a central concern of the international community.

The priorities of the United States section, which was formed in 1973, are disarmament, a just world order, the primacy of conscience, education for peace, and alternatives to violence. Pax Christi sections exist in 14 countries, with the international secretariat in Antwerp, Belgium. Its American address is 3000 N. Mango Ave., Chicago, IL 60634.

Unilateral Initiatives

In the spring of 1977, the Interchurch Peace Council in the Netherlands started work on a long-term campaign to remove nuclear arms from Dutch territory as a first step toward abolishing them altogether. The Interchurch Peace Council, an ecumenical group composed of representatives of Holland's major churches and religious bodies, developed a program around the slogan "Help rid the world of nuclear weapons; let it begin with the Netherlands."[5]

The idea was that if one country that relied on the nuclear umbrella could take the bold step of removing the umbrella because it posed a fundamental threat to the world, this action would spread to other nations. More and more of the world's peoples would press their leaders to abolish nuclear weapons if one nation took the lead.

The Interchurch Peace Council began its educational activities in the fall of 1977. Within a few months over 100 local groups became involved, increasing to more than 350 in the next 3 years.

By the early 1980's, it made Dutch participation in NATO nuclear programs an issue in every election. The country's Parliament voted not to allow new NATO missiles on Dutch soil. Several military officers resigned rather than carry out their nuclear assignments. The Peace Council's success inspired other advocates of European nuclear disarmament in a widespread wave of public demonstrations that some observers called Hollanditis.

Conclusion

The need Einstein saw for a new way of thinking to face the challenges of the nuclear age is met by an attitude of nonviolent peacemaking. Concern for meeting the needs of people, working for justice at every level, seeking to resolve all conflicts using active techniques of nonviolence, these are the components of the new thinking that is necessary to ensure the survival, and the success, of the human family.

For this process to be effective, the devil theory about those who maintain the current systems has to be avoided. These are not bad people who must be overcome. They are decent people with whom one can work.

Advocates of nuclear weapons are not steely-eyed, flint-hearted, power-mongerers, riding the heady crest of number one-ism, calloused to the wretched of the earth, and ready to kill to prove their manhood. It is possible to interpret the nuclear posture of the United States as a tragic mistake rather than as a symptom of a power-hungry, violence-prone society. It is possible to see most of those who support the possession of nuclear weapons as caring very much about liberty and justice, but taking the wrong means to achieve those grand goals.

Progressing beyond insults and cliches, peace people could help others recognize that the current age poses unique threats, and see the importance of exploring less violent means of preserving what ought to be preserved. Approaching others in love and concern, peace people can contribute to a healing process that allows a person the freedom to make the necessary changes.

Gandhi warned prophetically: "One thing is certain. If the mad race for armaments continues, it is bound to result in a slaughter such as has never occurred in history. . . . There is no escape from the impending doom save through a bold and unconditional acceptance of the nonviolent method with all its glorious implications."[6]

All the actions mentioned in this chapter call for continued, steady effort. The impetus toward increased weapons production and threat of their use is growing stronger rather than weaker. To slow down that momentum, then to reverse the trend, are long-term challenges. They will not succeed quickly. The normal American desire for fast solutions must be tempered with realism, American impatience with perseverance. The peace movement in the nuclear age is in for a long haul, hoping against hope that people can destroy the weapons before the weapons destroy the world.

Dutch Cardinal Bernard Alfrink sounded the call: "Across all frontiers we shall have to join forces and together exert ourselves to turn the tide. It seems to me that this is the greatest challenge of our times."

DISCUSSION QUESTIONS

The discussion questions for each chapter are intended to stimulate critical thinking and expanded understanding of the ideas discussed in the book. Some of them are included here because they have already been raised in response to public presentations of related material. Others have been the basis of college classroom discussions over several years.

Chapter 1

1. Why was the atomic bomb dropped on Japan? Under what circumstances would nuclear weapons be used today?

2. What effect would a one-megaton nuclear explosion have on the city where, or near where, you live?

3. When deterrences reach the "overkill" range, what results are effected by adding more nuclear weapons to a nation's arsenal?

4. Can the deliberate targeting of civilian population centers ever be morally right? Is it always wrong?

5. If you were close to the President of the United States during the Cuban missile crisis, what would you have advised him to do? What would you like the President to do in a similar crisis today?

Chapter 2

1. Why do you think the Old Testament was so strongly opposed to idolatry? Do you see any situations today where similar warnings would be appropriate?

2. What purpose was served by naming some of America's modern weapons after ancient, mythological gods?

3. Supporters of defense based on nuclear deterrence claim that it is the only practical, realistic approach in an age when other nations have these weapons. Could this reasoning be an instance of an "empty, rational philosophy based on the principles of this world" against which Saint Paul warned (Col. 2:6)? Explain your answer.

4. To what extent can you agree with Father McSorley's assertion that "It's a sin to build a nuclear weapon"? According to the same reasoning, what other activities connected with nuclear weapons would also be sinful?

Chapter 3

1. Jesus preached that the Kingdom of God is near. What would the Kingdom of God be like today? Describe it. Do you think it is still near?

2. Why was Jesus a threat to the established powers of his day? Would he be considered dangerous if he lived in a major city of the United States today?

3. Can you conceive of a situation where Caesar (the government) might require something contrary to God? How would you react to such a situation?

4. What positive guidance can you draw from the bible about how to handle conflicts?

5. The book of Revelation has often been interpreted as a prophecy about catastrophic events to come. Assuming that its principal purpose was to encourage Christians to remain faithful in time of persecution, what prophetic function can it still serve?

Chapter 4

1. "The most critical assumption underlying all nonviolent action is that both parties to the conflict share a common humanity" (p. 73). Do you think all people have at least a spark of human decency, or that some people are thoroughly bad, totally corrupt?

2. Martin Luther King, Jr. was widely criticized as a "troublemaker" when he employed some clearly defined nonviolent tactics such as marches, demonstrations, and boycotts. How would you answer that charge today?

3. What connection can you make between the nonviolent actions described in this chapter, and the life and teachings of Jesus?

Chapter 5

1. How can a person be a patriotic citizen of his or her own country, and a "world citizen" at the same time?

2. President Lincoln said, "I destroy my enemies when I make them my friends." Do you think it's possible to approach the problem of the Soviet Union along these lines? Explain your answer.

3. What practical steps can be taken to begin to create bonds of friendship between Americans and Soviet citizens? Have any such steps been taken already? With what results?

Chapter 6

1. Assuming that you are already involved in building a healthy spirituality, what sorts of things would you be inclined to study to pursue a degree of competence in critical areas in the Nuclear Age?

2. What are some examples of conflicts in daily life that could be effectively approached through nonviolent means?

3. How important do you think nonviolence is as a personal response to the challenge of the Nuclear Age?

4. What, concretely, are you going to do after reading this book?

NOTES

INTRODUCTION

1. Gil Elliot, *Twentieth Century Book of the Dead* (New York: Charles Scribner's Sons, 1972), pp. 83, 86.

2. Quoted in *Roots of War,* by Richard J. Barnet (Baltimore: Penguin Books, 1972), p. 111.

3. Quoted in *American Caesar: Douglas MacArthur 1880-1964,* by William Manchester (New York: Little, Brown and Co., 1978) Dell paperback edition, p. 16.

4. Address of September 18, 1967 to the editors of United Press International, in San Francisco.

Chapter 1

1. "Arms Control and Strategic Nuclear Forces," Statement by Secretary of State Alexander Haig before the Senate Foreign Relations Committee on Nov. 4, 1981, U.S. State Department, Bureau of Public Affairs, Current Policy No. 339, p. 2.

2. Statement by Secretary of Defense Harold Brown before the Senate Foreign Relations Committee on July 9, 1979.

3. Details on Japanese efforts to negotiate an end to the war, and on responses of the Allies, can be found in *The Rising Sun* by John Toland (New York: Random House, Bantam Book edition, 1970) pp. 848-54.

4. Henry L. Stimson, "The Decision to Use the Atomic Bomb," *Harper's* (February, 1947), excerpted in *Readings in World Politics,* by Robert A. Goldwin, second edition, revised by Tony Pearce (New York, Oxford University Press, 1970) p. 612.

5. Quoted in Toland, *The Rising Sun,* p. 764.

6. Quoted in *Christian Attitudes Toward War and Peace* by Roland H. Bainton (Nashville: Abingdon Press, 1960) p. 225.

7. Quoted in *War Through the Ages,* by Lynn Montross, rev. ed. (New York: Harper & Row, 1960) p. 920.

8. Quoted in Montross, *War Through the Ages,* p. 584.

9. Quoted in "The Morality of Obliteration Bombing," by John C. Ford, S.J., *Theological Studies,* 5 (1944), reprinted in *War and Morality,* by Richard A. Wasserstrom, ed. (Belmont, Calif.: Wadsworth Publishing Co., 1970) p. 31.

10. The bombing campaign against German cities is described in *The Destruction of Dresden* by David Irving (New York: Ballantine Books, 1963). See especially pp. 49, 67, 104, and 229.

11. Quoted in Irving, *The Destruction of Dresden,* p. 55.

12. John C. Ford, S.J., "The Morality of Obliteration Bombing," *Theological Studies,* 5 (1944), pp. 261-309.

13. Details on the development of the atomic bomb, including the Trinity test explosion, can be found in a 64-page booklet, *Los Alamos, Beginning of an Era 1943-45,* published by the Los Alamos Scientific Laboratory (no date).

14. The reactions of President Truman and Prime Minister Churchill, as well as the opinions of American military officials, are quoted in Toland, *The Rising Sun,* p. 867.

15. Quoted in Toland, *The Rising Sun,* p. 862.

16. Quoted in "The Atomic Bomb and American Foreign Policy, 1941-1945: An Historiographical Controversy" by Barton J. Bernstein, *Peace & Change,* Vol. II, No. 1 (Spring, 1974), p. 5.

17. Quoted in Toland, *The Rising Sun,* p. 865.

18. See Henry L. Stimson, "The Decision to Use the Atomic Bomb," *Harper's,* Feb. 1947, pp. 97-107.

19. Quoted in Toland, *The Rising Sun,* p. 877.

20. These three paragraphs containing eyewitness accounts are taken from 1) Bainton, *Christian Attitudes Toward War and Peace,* pp. 228-9; 2) *Give Me Water: Testimonies of Hiroshima and Nagasaki,* published by A Citizens' Group to Convey Testimonies of Hiroshima and Nagasaki (Tokyo, 1973) p. 8; and 3) in *Hiroshima Diary* by Michihiko Hachiya, excerpted in *Man and War,* edited by M. Jerry Weiss (New York: Dell Publishing Co., 1963) p. 247.

21. Quoted in Martin Caiden, *When War Comes* (New York: William Morrow and Co., 1972) p. 42.

22. Quoted in Toland, *The Rising Sun,* p. 891.

23. Albuquerque *Tribune,* Aug. 8, 1945, on display in the Atomic Museum, Kirkland Air Force Base, Albuquerque, New Mexico.

24. The last bombing raids on Japan are catalogued in "Shatterer of Worlds" by Barton J. Bernstein, *Bulletin of the Atomic Scientists,* December, 1975, p. 20. For the "big finale," see Toland, *The Rising Sun,* p. 950.

25. Bernstein, "The Atomic Bomb and American Foreign Policy, 1941-45: An Historiographical Controversy," p. 14.

26. "Robert Oppenheimer: the Los Alamos Years," Part Two, by Alice Kimball Smith and Charles Weiner, *Bulletin of the Atomic Scientists* (June 1980) p. 14.

27. Bernard T. Feld, "The Stake at SALT—Survival," *New York Times* (Dec. 9, 1970) p. 35.

28. Details of the consequences of a nuclear blast can be found in *The Effects of Nuclear War* by the Office of Technology Assessment, Congress of the United States (Montclair, N.J.: Allanheld, Ormun and Co., 1980).

29. Robert S. McNamara, *The Essence of Security* (New York: Harper & Row, 1968) pp. 53-4.

30. Quoted in "Deterrence by Means of Mass Destruction," by Herbert F. York, *Sane World* (May 1974) p. 58.

31. President Truman's press conference statement is quoted in *American Caesar: Douglas MacArthur 1880-1964* by William Manchester, p. 728. Secretary Dulles' offer is quoted in *The Indochina Story* by the Committee of Concerned Asian Scholars (New York: Bantam Books, 1970) p. 19. General Westmoreland's memoirs are quoted in *America in Vietnam* by Guenter Lewy (New York: Oxford University Press, 1978) p. 128.

32. Robert F. Kennedy, *Thirteen Days: A Memoir of the Cuban Missile Crisis* (New York: Norton, 1969).

33. Daniel Lang, "The Supreme Option," *The New Yorker* (Jan. 9, 1971) p. 55.

34. William V. O'Brien, "Legitimate Military Necessity in Nuclear War," in *World Polity,* Vol. II, (Washington, D.C.: Georgetown University, The Institute of World Polity, 1960) p. 79.

35. The nuclear threat and the urgent necessity to respond creatively to it are described at length in *The Fate of the World,* by Jonathan Schell (New York: Alfred A. Knopf, 1982).

Chapter 2

1. Pastoral Constitution on the Church in the Modern World *(Gaudium et Spes),* 79.

2. For an analysis of the money projected for defense in the period 1981-86, see *The Defense Monitor* 10, No. 3 (Washington, D.C.: The Center for Defense Information, 1981). Also "1983 Military Budget" by John Isaacs, *Bulletin of the Atomic Scientists* (April 1982) pp. 16-18.

3. This and the following descriptions of U.S. weapons are taken from a variety of sources, including the annual *Defense Department Reports* submitted to Congress each year with the budget requests, and a series of publications by the National Strategy Information Center, e.g., *Strategic Weapons: An Introduction* by Norman Polman (New York: Crane, Russak and Co., 1975).

4. Names and activities of the ancient gods can be found in sources such as the *New Larousse Encyclopedia of Mythology* (Middlesex, England: Hamlyn House, 1968) and the *Smaller Classical Dictionary* by Sir William Smith (New York: E.P. Dutton and Co., 1958).

5. All Scripture quotations in this chapter are taken from *The Jerusalem Bible* (New York: Doubleday and Co., 1966).

6. Pastoral Constitution on the Church in the Modern World *(Gaudium et Spes),* 81.

7. This alert was cited in "Mobilizing for Survival" by Sidney Lens, originally published in *Washington Watch,* reprinted in the *Sojourners Peace Packet,* Part 1, 1978. The following two incidents, like this one, were widely reported in the press—e.g., "How Computer Erred on Nuclear Alert," *Chicago Tribune,* Nov. 18, 1979, Sec. 1, p. 3, and "Fake Missile Alarms Tied to Tiny Circuit," *The Commercial Appeal,* Memphis, Tennessee (June 18, 1980) p. 10.

8. Richard J. Barnet, "A Time to Stop," in *The Nuclear Arms Race* (Washington, D.C.: Sojourners, *Peace Packet, Part 1,* 1978) p. 2.

9. Father Richard McSorley's article "It's a Sin to Build a Nuclear Weapon" first appeared in *U.S. Catholic* (October 1976) pp. 12 ff.

10. A complete account of Daniel Berrigan's testimony can be found in "The Push of Conscience," in *Sojourners* (June 1981) pp. 20-23.

Chapter 3

1. For an analysis of Jesus' reaction to the political situation in his homeland, see *Jesus, Politics and Society* by Richard J. Cassidy (Maryknoll, N.Y.: Orbis Books, 1978) especially chapters 3 and 4.

2. A description of Roman military forces and occupation tactics can be found in historical sources such as *War Through The Ages* by Lynn Montross, rev. ed. (New York: Harper & Row, 1960) especially chapter 4; and *Rome: The Story of an Empire,* by J.P.V.D. Balsdom (New York: McGraw-Hill, 1970).

3. Montross, *War Through the Ages,* p. 51.

4. This incident is reported in *The Politics of Love* by John Ferguson (Cambridge, England: James Clarke Publishers) (no date), pp. 76-77.

5. Josephus' full description is given in *The Politics of Jesus* by John Howard Yoder (Grand Rapids: Eerdmans, 1972) p. 91.

6. All Scripture quotations in this chapter are taken from the *New International Version* (Grand Rapids, Mich.: Zondervan, 1973).

7. For a more detailed analysis of Jesus' counter-cultural approaches, see *Jesus in Bad Company* by Adolf Holl (New York: Holt, Rinehart and Winston, 1973).

8. Paul's attitude toward the Roman Empire and its laws is clarified in many sources, e.g., *The Power and the Wisdom* by John L. McKenzie (Milwaukee: Bruce Publishing Co., 1965) chapter XII.

9. This and the following two prayers are found in *Man Seeks the Divine* by Edwin A. Burtt (New York: Harper & Row, 1957) p. 36.

Chapter 4

1. See M.K. Gandhi, *An Autobiography* (Boston: Beacon Press, 1972) pp. 275, and 349-50; also *Non-Violent Resistance* by Gandhi (New York: Schocken Books, 1971) pp. 40-42.

2. Thomas Merton, *Faith and Violence* (Notre Dame: University of Notre Dame Press, 1968) p. 25.

3. See Gordon Zahn, *An Alternative to War* (New York: Council on Religion and International Affairs, 1963) p. 11, for this analysis of the dynamics of nonviolence.

4. Gene Sharp, *The Politics of Nonviolent Action* (Boston: Porter Sargent Publishers, 1973) pp. xii-xvi.

5. Quoted in *Conquest of Violence* by Joan V. Bondurant (Berkeley: University of California Press, 1965) p. 17.

6. Carl Von Clausewitz, *On War* (Baltimore: Penguin Books edition, 1968) p. 119.

7. Gene Sharp, "Disregarded History: The Power of Nonviolent Action," *Fellowship* (March 1976) pp. 7-8.

8. Quoted in *The Psychology of Nonviolence,* by Leroy H. Pelton (New York: Pergamon Press, 1974) p. 1.

9. Martin Luther King, Jr., *Why We Can't Wait* (New York: New American Library, 1964) p. 152.

10. Quoted by Gordon Zahn in his Introduction to *Thomas Merton on Peace* (New York: McCall, 1972) p. xxix.

Chapter 5

1. Pierre Teilhard de Chardin, S.J., *Building the Earth* (Wilkes-Barre, Pa.: Dimension Books, 1965) p. 43. The other quotations of Teilhard de Chardin in this chapter are found in the same book, pp. 43-55.

2. Quoted in *Roots of War* by Richard J. Barnet, p. 87.

3. Quoted in *War and Peace in the World's Religions,* by John Ferguson (New York: Oxford University Press, 1978) p. 48.

4. *The Autobiography of Malcolm X* (New York: Grove Press, 1964) p. 338.

5. Quoted by Sidney Lens in his article "Thirty Years of Escalation," *The Nation* (May 27, 1978) pp. 623-4.

6. Quoted in Bainton, *Christian Attitudes Toward War and Peace,* p. 125.

7. Gerald and Patricia Mische, *Toward a Human World Order* (Ramsey, N.J.: Paulist Press, 1977) p. 351.

8. Rene Dubos, "Unity through Diversity," in *Who Speaks for Earth?* (New York: Norton, 1973) p. 42.

9. Quoted in "Notes and Comment," *The New Yorker,* March 4, 1974, p. 27.

10. "The Princeton Declaration," published by the World Conference on Religion and Peace, New York, 1979.

11. Pastoral Constitution on the Church in the Modern World *(Gaudium et Spes),* #75.

12. Morton Deutsch, *The Resolution of Conflict* (New Haven: Yale University Press, 1973) p. 68.

13. President Carter at the Georgia Institute of Technology in Atlanta on February 20, 1979; U.S. State Department, Bureau of Public Affairs, Current Policy No. 57.

14. Robert G. Kaiser, "The Arms Race: A Soviet View," in *The Nuclear Arms Race* (Washington, D.C.: Sojourners, *Peace Packet, Part 1,* 1978) p. 19.

15. Richard J. Barnet, "U.S.-Soviet Relations: The Need for a Comprehensive Approach," in *Foreign Affairs* (Spring 1979) p. 783.

16. *Instead of Violence,* edited by Arthur and Lila Weinburg (Boston: Beacon Press, 1968) p. 123.

Chapter 6

1. Most of the positions summarized in this section can be found in *Man and Aggression,* edited by Ashley Montagu (New York: Oxford University Press, 1968).

2. The complete story of this incident is found in "Meeting at Our Roots: A Conversation with Joseph Abileah" by Jim Forest, in *IFOR Reports* (Alkmaar, Netherlands, December 1980) pp. 4-8.

3. Joseph J. Fahey, "The Moral Challenge of Peace Education," in *Journal of Peace Studies* (New York: Manhattan College, Vol. 1, No. 1, 1976) p. 1.

4. Robert McAfee Brown, *Making Peace in the Global Village* (Philadelphia: Westminster, 1981) p. 15.

5. Details of the Interchurch Peace Council's campaign can be found in "A Contagion of Peace," by Jim Forest and Peter Herby, and "New Life in Dry Bones," by Jim Forest, both in *Sojourners* (February 1982).

6. Mahatma Gandhi, *All Men Are Brothers* (Ahmedabad, India: Navajivan Publishing House, 1960) p. 159.

SELECTED BIBLIOGRAPHY

Bainton, Roland H. *Christian Attitudes Toward War and Peace.* Nashville, Tenn.: Abington Press, 1960.

Barnet, Richard J. *Roots of War.* Baltimore: Penguin Books, 1972.

Berrigan, Daniel. *Ten Commandments for the Long Haul.* Nashville, Tenn: Abingdon Press, 1981.

Brown, Robert McAfee. *Peacemaking in the Global Village.* Philadelphia: Westminster, 1981.

Cassidy, Richard J. *Jesus, Politics and Society.* Maryknoll, N.Y.: Orbis Books, 1978.

Douglass, James W. *The Non-Violent Cross.* New York: Macmillan, 1966.

Dozier, Bishop Carroll T. Pastoral Letter "Peace: Gift and Task," *Commonweal,* (December 24, 1971) 289, 294-300.

Ellul, Jacques. *Violence.* New York: Seabury Press, 1969.

Fahey, Joseph J. *Peace, War and the Christian Conscience.* New York: The Christophers, 1982.

Ferguson, John. *The Politics of Love.* Cambridge, England: James Clarke Publishers (no date).

————. *War and Peace in the World's Religions.* New York: Oxford University Press, 1978.

Furfey, Paul Hanly. *The Respectable Murderers.* New York: Herder and Herder, 1966.

Gandhi, Mohandas K. *An Autobiography.* Boston: Beacon Press, 1972.

————. *Non-Violent Resistance.* New York: Schocken Books, 1971.

Gregg, Richard B. *The Power of Nonviolence.* London: James Clarke, 1960.

Gremillon, Joseph. *The Gospel of Peace and Justice.* Maryknoll, N.Y.: Orbis Books, 1976.

Hersey, John. *Hiroshima.* New York: Bantam Books, 1966.

Hope, Marjorie, and James Young. *The Struggle for Humanity.* Maryknoll, N.Y.: Orbis Books, 1977.

IDOC International. *The Security Trap.* Geneva, Switzerland: World Council of Churches, 1979.

King, Martin Luther, Jr. *Strength to Love.* New York: Pocket Books, 1968.

————. *Why We Can't Wait.* New York: New American Library, 1964.

Lynd, Staughton, ed. *Nonviolence in America: A Documentary History.* New York: Bobbs-Merrill, 1966.

128

McSorley, Georgetown
Univer.
_____. *New Testament Basis of Pacifism.* Washington, D.C.: George-
town University, Center for Peace Studies, 1979.
Merton, Thomas. *Faith and Violence.* Notre Dame, Ind.: U. of Notre
Dame Press, 1968.
Miller, William Robert. *Nonviolence: A Christian Interpretation.* New
York: Schocken Books, 1966.
Mische, Gerald and Patricia. *Toward a Human World Order.* Ramsey,
N.J.: Paulist Press, 1977.
Office of Technology Assessment. *The Effects of Nuclear War.* Montclair,
N.J.: Allanheld, Osmun, 1980.
Pelton, Leroy. *The Psychology of Nonviolence.* New York: Pergamon
Press, 1974.
Regamey, Pie, O.P. *Non-Violence and the Christian Conscience.* New
York: Herder and Herder, 1966.
Samuel, Dorothy T. *Safe Passage on City Streets.* Nashville, Tenn.: Abing-
don Press, 1975.
Schell, Jonathan. *The Fate of the World.* New York: Alfred A. Knopf,
1982.
Shannon, Thomas A., ed. *War or Peace? The Search for New Answers.*
Maryknoll, N.Y.: Orbis Books, 1980.
Sharp, Gene. *Making the Abolition of War a Realistic Goal.* New York: In-
stitute for World Order, 1981.
_____. *The Politics of Nonviolent Action.* Boston: Porter Sargent Pub-
lishers, 1973.
Teilhard de Chardin, Pierre, S.J. *Building the Earth.* Wilkes-Barre, Pa.:
Dimension Books, 1965.
_____. *The Future of Man.* New York, Harper & Row: 1964.
Toland, John. *The Rising Sun: The Decline and Fall of the Japanese Em-
pire.* New York: Random House, 1970.
United Reformed Church. *Non-Violent Action.* London: SCM Press, 1973.
Vanderhaar, Gerard A. *Nonviolence: Theory and Practice.* Chicago: Pax
Christi USA, 1982.
Jim Wallis. *The Call to Conversion.* New York: Harper & Row, 1981.
Weinberg, Arthur and Lila, eds. *Instead of Violence.* Boston: Beacon
Press, 1968.
Yoder, John Howard. *The Politics of Jesus.* Grand Rapids, Mich.: Eerd-
mans, 1972.
Zahn, Gordon. *An Alternative to War.* New York: Council on Religion and
International Affairs, 1963.
_____. *In Solitary Witness: the Life and Death of Franz Jagerstatter.*
Boston: Beacon Press, 1964.
_____. *Thomas Merton on Peace.* New York: McCall, 1971.